Sparkle & Shine

TEEN DEVOTIONAL FOR GIRLS

STRENGTHEN RELATIONSHIPS
MANAGE ANXIETY, AND
EMBRACE GOD'S LOVE DAILY

Graceful Growth

Contents

READER BONUS

Follow the Steps Below to Claim Your Free Copy of "Life Skills for Teens and Young Adults Revolution"

Prepare for adulthood with this essential guide to mastering life skills for a successful and fulfilling future.

- **Overcome Uncertainty:** Transform doubt into confidence.

- **Gain Independence**: Learn essential life skills to navigate adulthood.

- **Embrace Opportunities:** Pursue your dreams without fear.

STEP 1: LEAVE A REVIEW (OPTIONAL)

It would mean a lot to me if you could leave a quick review for

"Sparkle & Shine, Teen Devotional for Girls!"

Scan below!

Step 2: Claim Your Bonus

Claim your free bonus by scanning the QR code.

Just tell us where to send it!

Equip yourself with the skills to thrive in adulthood!

Don't wait—get your free eBook now!

How to Create My Prayer Journal >>

Introduction

Do you ever scroll through social media and feel like everyone else is thriving while you're struggling to get through the day? You're not alone. Every heart emoji and perfect selfie can make it seem like you're the only one struggling to find your place and purpose. But here's the truth: behind every filtered photo, there are real challenges—just like yours—waiting to be met with courage and hope.

That's why I wrote "Sparkle & Shine: Teen Devotional for Girls: Strengthen Relationships, Manage Anxiety, and Embrace God's Love Daily."

This book invites you to explore the powerful themes of overcoming, managing, and embracing. It's about finding your *sparkle amidst* and shining with a light that's uniquely yours, grounded in faith and love.

I began writing this book one sunny afternoon at a local coffee shop, watching a group of teens at the following table. They laughed with lively joy, but their conversation carried undertones of stress about appearances, acceptance, and the fear of missing out. I realized how much things had changed yet stayed the same since my teenage years. I felt a solid call to reach out and offer a lifeline of truth and encouragement through the difficulties of teen life.

"Sparkle & Shine" is structured to walk with you, day by day, through personal stories, biblical insights, and practical advice. Each chapter builds on the last, creating a journey of growth and discovery. From tackling the tough topics of self-image and peer pressure to fostering a deep, personal relationship with God, this book is a comprehensive guide for daily challenges and triumphs.

Throughout the book, you'll find interactive elements like journal prompts to reflect on your experiences, prayers to connect with God, and challenges encouraging you to practice what you've learned. These tools help you engage more deeply with each topic and apply the lessons to your life.

As each page is turned, remember: You are not alone on your journey. Every step you take equips you with the faith and confidence to navigate life's complexities. Together, we'll uncover the beauty of who you are and empower you to *sparkle and shine* in every area of your life.

Let's start this adventure, shall we?

Chapter 1

Embracing Your
True Self in Christ

Do you ever wonder who you are beneath all the labels and expectations? In a world filled with so many voices telling you who you should be, it can feel overwhelming to uncover your true self. What if I told you that embracing your uniqueness is more important than conforming to societal expectations? This chapter delves into finding your true, God-given identity by shedding societal expectations.

1.1. Designed Uniquely: Exploring Your God-Given Identity

Every one of us is a masterpiece intricately designed by God. Psalms 139:13-14 sings a song of our creation, reminding us we are **"fearfully and wonderfully made."** These words aren't just beautiful poetry but the foundation of understanding our value and purpose. God doesn't mass-produce us. He crafted each of us distinctively, with unique talents, personalities, and paths in life. Like snowflakes dancing down from the sky, we each have our distinct pattern as we walk on this earth.

However, a society that often values conformity can cloud this truth. The world tries to fit us into boxes—defining worth by likes and superficial standards that change with the seasons. Feeling lost in the shuffle and disconnected from who we are is effortless. But here's the empowering truth: These shifting sands don't determine your worth. The Bible offers a rock-solid foundation for your identity. When feelings of inadequacy creep in, remember that your Creator created you with intention and purpose. He deeply loves and values you just as He designed you.

To dive deeper into this understanding, consider these journal prompts to start your exploration:

What are the unique traits that make you, you?

How do these reflect God's creativity?

What pressures do you feel to conform, and how do they affect your sense of self?

Are these pressures aligned with or distracting from God's intentions for you?

Writing your thoughts can be a powerful way to affirm your God-given identity and see yourself as He sees you.

Let's also draw inspiration from others who have walked this path. Take, for instance, Sarah, a teen who struggled with her self-image. Through prayer and reflection on scriptures that affirm her identity in God, she saw herself as more than her achievements or failures. She shared, "Learning that God crafted me changed everything. I started to value myself not for what I do but for who I am in Him." Sarah's journey is a testament to the transformative power of embracing one's divine design.

Reflective Exercise:

To solidify this concept, try this reflective exercise: Create a "Truths About Me" board.

Gather a piece of poster board and some markers, then write down truths about your identity based on Scripture, like "I am a child of God" (John 1:12) or "I am created with purpose" (Ephesians 2:10). Decorate it with images or designs that speak to you. Place your board somewhere you will see it daily as a reminder of who you are in Christ.

As you continue through this chapter, remember that embracing your unique design and grounding your identity in Christ allows you to step into the freedom of being your true self, unswayed by the world. Keep peeling back the layers, discovering more about the incredible person God made you to be. Remember, in His eyes, you are a masterpiece, and that's something worth celebrating.

1.2 MIRROR, MIRROR: CONFRONTING BEAUTY STANDARDS WITH BIBLICAL TRUTH

In today's society, the mirror often reflects more than just our physical appearance; it reflects the pressures and ideals imposed by the media and popular culture. These beauty standards are not only fleeting but are also incredibly narrow. Defining beauty in such limited terms makes it nearly impossible for most of us to meet them. However, when we turn to the Bible, we find a vastly different narrative about beauty—enduring and inclusive.

For instance, when we look at heroines like Esther and Sarah, we see that their beauty is not merely about their physical appearance. Take Esther as an example - she was unquestionably beautiful, but her natural beauty radiated from her bravery and wisdom in handling complicated political dynamics to protect her people. Similarly, Sarah's beauty was part of her story, but her faith and resilience stood out, especially as she embraced the role of a mother of nations in her old age.

The societal lens often distorts what true beauty entails. It focuses on the external while neglecting the internal qualities that make each of us unique and beautiful. To shift this focus, it's crucial to consciously take steps to redefine what beauty means on a personal level.

Challenging ourselves with a media fast is a practical step we can take. It doesn't have to be long, a day or a weekend.

The goal is to temporarily remove the streams of images and messages that often bombard us with unrealistic beauty standards. During this time, you can reflect on the qualities that define you beyond your appearance. Another step is to curate your social media feeds by actively choosing to follow accounts that promote a healthy and diverse view of beauty. Look for content that uplifts and reflects the true diversity of God's creation rather than those that perpetuate narrow ideals.

Furthermore, believing that your body is a sacred dwelling of the Holy Spirit (1 Corinthians 6:19-20) can significantly alter your self-perception. This Scripture isn't just about health or purity; it's about respect and reverence for the craftsmanship of God. Seeing your body as a sacred dwelling place for the Holy Spirit shifts your focus from societal approval to divine appreciation. This perspective fosters a more profound respect for yourself and challenges superficial judgments based on appearance alone. It emphasizes the importance of caring for your body to meet external ideals and show gratitude to its Creator.

Let's consider the stories of young women who have embraced these practices. Many recount how stepping back from constant media exposure allowed them to reconnect with their authentic selves and appreciate aspects of their beauty they had overlooked or undervalued. They speak of the freedom to release the pressure to conform to unattainable standards and discover a more profound beauty rooted in their character and spiritual life. This transformation isn't only about feeling better now; it's about a lasting change in how they perceive themselves and others.

When we reshape our concept of beauty to align with God's, we invite a world where every reflection in the mirror emanates strength, dignity, and divine artistry. This realignment is not a rejection of physical beauty but an invitation to celebrate a more holistic and inclusive beauty that honors our Creator and the true essence of who we are. As you continue this path, let the mirror reflect who you are: beautifully and wonderfully made, cherished, and adorned by God.

1.3 'I am Enough': Understanding Your Value in Christ

Let's talk about a truth that can sometimes feel slippery in the hustle of daily pressures and expectations: your intrinsic value. It stays the same with your grades, social status, and even the number of likes on your Instagram post. This value has a deep and eternal foundation. As God's children, we find our true worth in being loved and redeemed by Christ, not in our fleeting achievements or the ever-changing opinions of others.

Understanding that you are "enough" involves embracing that your value comes from God. Understanding this allows you to break free from the constant pursuit of approval or perfection. In Romans 5:8, we find a profound statement of our worth: **"But God demonstrates His love for us in this: While we were still sinners, Christ died for us."** This means our value is so great to God that He was willing to give His only Son to ensure our salvation and freedom. God did not wait for us to become perfect; He took action out of His immense love for us, flawed and all.

But amid the chaos of being a teenager, it's easy to believe the lies that say you're not good enough, smart enough, or popular enough. These lies can distort your self-image and make you feel as though your value is something you need to earn. But here's the truth to hold on to 2 Corinthians 5:17 tells us, **"Therefore, if anyone is in Christ, the new creation has come: The old has gone, the new is here!"** You are continuously renewed by God's grace, not by your efforts. You are enough because God says you are, and He is continually working within you to bring about His perfect plan for your life.

To help reinforce this truth in your heart, here are some key verses to memorize and recall whenever you feel doubts creeping in about your worth:

- **Isaiah 43:1:** "Do not fear, for I have redeemed you; I have summoned you by name; you are mine."

- **Jeremiah 29:11**: "For I know the plans I have for you," declares the LORD, "plans to prosper you and not to harm you, plans to give you hope and a future."

- **Zephaniah 3:17**: "The LORD your God is with you, the Mighty Warrior who saves. He will delight you greatly; in His love, He will no longer rebuke you but rejoice over you with singing."

The scriptures provide stability when doubt and insecurity threaten to overwhelm you. Write them down, keep them on your phone, pin them on your room's wall—keep them where they can remind you daily of your unshakeable value in Christ.

Now, let us come together in a guided prayer focus, seeking God's affirmation and asking for help in seeing ourselves as He sees us:

"Dear Heavenly Father, I come before You today, grateful for Your unconditional love and mercy. Sometimes, I find it hard to believe that I am enough. I look at myself and see the flaws and the mistakes. But today, I choose to see myself through Your eyes. Help me to grasp the depth of Your love and the truth that I am a new creation in Christ. Remind me that my value comes from You and not from anything I can achieve alone. Teach me to rest in the truth that I am cherished, loved, and enough because You say I am. Thank you for seeing me as worth dying for, even on my hardest days. In Jesus' Name, Amen."

Embracing this prayer and the truths from Scripture can guide your heart to a place of peace and acceptance. Remember, you are enough in God's eyes—not because of your actions, but due to His grace. Let this assurance sink deeply into your heart, and watch how it transforms how you view yourself and your interactions with others. Keep these truths close to your heart and allow them to navigate you through each day, knowing with certainty that you are always worthy in Christ.

1.4 Overcoming the Comparison Trap on Social Media

Scrolling through Instagram or TikTok, it's easy to feel like everyone else has a perfect life. You see endless streams of vacation photos, flawless selfies, and achievements celebrated with exuberance. It's natural to compare your everyday life to these highlight reels, but remember, social media is often a curated display, not a representation of real life. This digital distortion can lead to inadequacy and a persistent sense of falling short. Recognizing that each post is just a fragment of a person's life, not the whole story, is essential.

The story of Leah and Rachel in Genesis 29-30 provides a poignant biblical perspective on the perils of comparison. Leah and Rachel were sisters, each desiring what the other had.

Leah longed for the love Rachel received from Jacob, while Rachel envied Leah's ability to bear children. Their story illustrates how comparison can lead to discontent and strife, even among loved ones. Instead of focusing on what they lacked, imagine if they had celebrated each other's unique blessings. The Bible teaches us to find peace in our unique paths, recognizing that our value comes from God, not from earthly achievements or recognition.

To navigate social media healthily, start by setting boundaries for your usage. Limiting your time on these platforms can reduce the urge to compare. Try setting a daily limit—perhaps an hour a day, broken into manageable intervals—to engage with social media. Use an app to monitor your usage and hold yourself accountable to these limits. This practice helps create a balance, allowing you to enjoy social media's benefits without letting it overwhelm your life.

Ensure your feed reflects positivity and inspiration through curation. Follow accounts that uplift and encourage you, whether they're spiritual leaders, motivational speakers, or friends who share encouraging content. Unfollow or mute accounts that trigger feelings of inadequacy or comparison. Doing so isn't about cutting people out of your life; it's simply protecting your mental space.

Social media should be a tool for connection and inspiration, not a source of stress.

Lastly, focus on creating a positive online presence. Share posts that reflect your true self and your faith. These could include a Bible verse that inspired you, a personal challenge you've overcome, or how you navigate the pressure of comparison. By being authentic, you encourage others to do the same, creating a ripple effect of positivity. Using social media to uplift others enhances your experience and contributes to a healthier online community.

However, it's essential to remember that sharing your faith online can sometimes attract negativity or unwanted comments. If you receive pushback or encounter negativity, remember to stand firm in your convictions and pray for those who respond with hostility. It's common to face harassment on biblical posts, but don't let it deter you. If fitting in on social media is a sensitive area for you, drawing negative attention could feel discouraging. In those moments, remind yourself that your worth is grounded in God's love, not others' opinions. Focus on sharing what is true to you, and don't engage with negativity.

By applying these biblical insights and practical tips, you can transform your social media experience from a source of stress to a space of encouragement and self-expression. Remember, the goal isn't to portray a perfect life but to connect and grow in a way that enriches your life and aligns with your faith. As you explore the digital realm, use its powerful tools wisely, forming authentic and positive connections.

1.5 GOD'S MASTERPIECE: LEARNING TO LOVE YOUR BODY AS GOD DOES

In a world that often demands a specific appearance for beauty, accepting that we are fearfully and wonderfully made, as Psalm 139:14 states, is revolutionary. This acceptance isn't just a nice thought; it's a declaration of divine truth about our physical bodies. Every curve, every freckle, every hair on our heads is made with intention and care. Our bodies are diverse, reflecting the immense creativity of God, who delights in variety and uniqueness. Think about the world's vastness, landscapes, climates, and ecosystems, all crafted by the same Creator who designed you. Just as a sunset doesn't need to lose weight or a mountain doesn't need to clear its skin, you are perfect in your natural, God-given form.

Nevertheless, it can be challenging to embrace this reality, especially when confronted with the harshness of body shaming. It's a toxic practice that harms the individual and perpetuates a culture of negativity and judgment. Speaking poorly about our bodies or others' doesn't align with the love and respect we are called to show as followers of Christ. Instead, we are encouraged to speak life into ourselves and those around us. Imagine replacing a critical word with a kind one—consider how that might change how you feel about yourself and influence those who hear it. By choosing to celebrate our bodies as God's handiwork, we actively reject the lies that seek to undermine our self-worth.

Let's incorporate practices that align with this mindset to foster a healthier relationship with our bodies. Keeping a gratitude journal focused on the functional aspects of your body can be very impactful. This journal can be a simple daily record where you jot down things like, 'Today, I'm thankful for my legs that carried me everywhere I needed to go,' or 'I'm grateful for my eyes that allowed me to see the beauty of the day.

The transition from valuing appearance to valuing functionality and gratitude can profoundly affect our self-perception and enhance our appreciation for our bodies' remarkable capabilities.

God used figures in the Bible mightily, regardless of their physical characteristics. Consider Moses, who was slow of speech, or Paul, who spoke of a physical thorn in his flesh. Their stories are not of physical perfection but of faith and obedience that transcended their physical limitations. Moses led a nation to freedom, and Paul spread the gospel worldwide. Their physical condition didn't hinder their effectiveness; instead, their faith and the strength of God empowered them. Their lives remind us that our value and capacity to be used by God are not dependent on meeting any human standard of physical perfection but are rooted in our faith and actions.

When we embrace this viewpoint, we break free from the ceaseless expectations to fit into ever-changing beauty norms and instead discover a more profound beauty and sense of purpose in embracing our true selves.

As we navigate the messages the world throws at us, let's hold fast to the affirmations of our worth and beauty in Scripture. Let's see ourselves and each other through the lens of God's love, a love that celebrates diversity, cherishes individuality, and empowers us to live confidently in the bodies we've been given. Remember, in God's eyes, and indeed in truth, you are His masterpiece, crafted with purpose and destined for greatness. Let this truth sink in and free you from doubt about your physical appearance. Live out your God-given potential, making a difference in the world based on who you are in Him, not your appearance.

1.6 The Power of Positive Self-Talk: Affirmations from Scripture

Words are powerful tools. They can build up or tear down, inspire hope, or invoke despair. Proverbs 18:21 tells us, **'The tongue has the power of life and death,'** highlighting the significant impact our words can have on our lives and the lives of others. The effect is incredibly profound when considering the words we speak to ourselves. Every day, whether or not we're aware of it, we're engaged in self-talk, and the nature of these internal conversations can significantly influence our mindset and faith. Negative self-talk can spiral into a destructive pattern that pulls us away from seeing ourselves as God sees us. Conversely, positive self-talk, rooted in the truths of Scripture, can uplift and affirm our identity in Christ, reinforcing a healthy, God-centered view of ourselves.

Developing a habit of positive self-talk isn't about ignoring the realities of life's challenges but about approaching them with a mindset that aligns with God's truth. It's about replacing lies and doubts with affirmations of faith, strength, and victory. For example, instead of getting stuck in a loop of thinking, "I can't handle this," you could affirm, **"I can do all things through Christ who strengthens me"** (Philippians 4:13). This shift doesn't happen overnight. It requires deliberate practice and mindfulness. Start by becoming more aware of your internal dialogue. Take note of when negative thoughts arise, like during a test, a difficult conversation, or even when you look at yourself in the mirror. Recognizing these moments is the first step to transforming them.

Scripture offers a treasure trove of affirmations to fortify and renew your mind. Here are a few to integrate into your daily routine:

- **"I am fearfully and wonderfully made"** (Psalm 139:14). This affirmation is a powerful reminder of your divine creation and unique beauty.

- **"For I know the plans I have for you, declares the Lord, plans for welfare and not for evil, to give you a future and a hope"** (Jeremiah 29:11). This promise can be a comforting assurance during times of uncertainty or fear.

- **"I am a child of God"** (John 1:12). This simple yet profound truth can help reinforce your identity and belonging in Christ.

Make these affirmations part of your daily rhythm. You might recite them during your morning routine, write them on sticky notes around your room, or repeat them in your mind during challenging moments. The key is consistency. The more you fill your mind with God's truths, the more natural they will feel, replacing the negative patterns that once held sway.

If you want to put these principles into practice:

1. Keep a daily log of moments when you notice yourself engaging in negative self-talk.

2. Document the situation and the specific thoughts that arose.

3. Take a moment to reframe these thoughts by writing a corresponding scriptural affirmation.

For example, if you noted, "I'm not smart enough to figure this out," you could reframe it to, **"God gives me wisdom generously when I ask for it,"** based on James 1:5. This exercise not only helps in recognizing and halting negative self-talk but also in embedding scriptural truths more deeply into your thought processes.

Positive self-talk based on scriptural truths is not just about boosting self-esteem; it's a spiritual discipline that aligns your thoughts with God's Word, empowering you to live out your faith more fully. It fortifies your spiritual armor, equipping you to face the challenges of teenage life with confidence and peace. Remember, the goal here is not to achieve perfection in your thoughts but to grow in grace and truth, allowing God's Word to reshape and uplift your heart and mind.

As you continue to practice and integrate these affirmations into your life, you'll notice a shift in how you view yourself and your circumstances. This shift goes beyond just feeling better—it's about living in the freedom and truth that Christ offers. It's about walking in the identity He has given you, a loved, valued, and purposeful identity.

ACTIVITY - CHAPTER 1

Scan the QR code.

Chapter 2

Navigating Relationships with Grace

Have you ever thought about how much your friendships shape your journey? Picture your life as a garden, with relationships like the growing plants. Some friendships are like beautiful flowers that bring joy and color, while others might be like weeds that need careful tending or even removal. Just like a gardener cares for her garden, you can nurture relationships that enrich your life and align with your faith. This chapter will help you cultivate a garden of fulfilling friendships rooted in God's love and wisdom.

2.1 CHOOSING FRIENDS WISELY: QUALITIES OF GODLY FRIENDSHIPS

Not all friendships are created equal. Think about the story of David and Jonathan in the Bible. Their friendship displayed deep loyalty, mutual respect, and an unshakeable bond rooted in their faith in God. Jonathan, who was supposed to be a rival for the throne, supported David even when it meant risking his position and safety. This kind of friendship goes beyond surface-level interactions; it deepens into commitment and genuine care. Choosing friends wisely, with faith as your guide, helps you build a social circle that aligns with your faith and values.

Loyalty is one essential quality of a godly friendship—it's about being there for your friend no matter what. Just like Jonathan stood by David through thick and thin, a loyal friend supports you during victories and struggles. Honesty is another pillar; it involves being truthful, even when it's hard, and sharing insights that help each other grow. Lastly, there's a shared commitment to faith. While you might not agree on every detail, encouraging each other to grow closer to God strengthens your bond.

However, we must be aware of our friends' influence on us. The Bible warns us in 1 Corinthians 15:33, "Do not be misled: **Bad company corrupts good character.**" It isn't about judging others but recognizing how close relationships impact our choices and faith. If a friendship pulls you away from your values, it might be time to reconsider its place in your life. It doesn't mean cutting people off recklessly; it's about being mindful of who you let into your inner circle—those with regular access to your heart and mind.

To find enriching friendships, look for communities that promote spiritual growth, like a church youth group, a Christian club at school, or a Bible study group. These environments can help you meet peers seeking to live out their faith and understand your challenges. These groups provide fertile ground for friendships that encourage your walk with God and inspire you to grow spiritually.

Spiritual Accountability in Friendships

The idea of **"iron sharpening iron,"** from Proverbs 27:17, is a cornerstone of godly friendships. These are friends who are not afraid to challenge and support your spiritual development. They love you enough to point out when you might be veering off course and cheer you on when you're doing well. Just as iron blades sharpen each other through friction, the loving and sometimes challenging feedback from a good friend helps sharpen your character.

Open communication is vital for building this kind of accountability. Establish trust and respect from the start, letting your friends know they can speak truthfully to you and that you're committed to doing the same for them. You might have regular check-ins where you discuss more meaningful topics than just the latest gossip or your favorite shows. Instead, share your struggles, victories, doubts, and discoveries. Being open in this way creates a strong support network that allows everyone to grow spiritually and personally, empowering you and fostering a deeper connection with your friends.

Building these kinds of friendships isn't just about improving your social life; it's about deepening your faith and helping others do the same. These relationships become a circle of support, challenge, and encouragement, helping you flourish socially and spiritually. Remember, as you navigate the complexities of teenage friendships, being around people who bring you closer to God and fill your life with laughter and love is crucial.

2.2 Dealing with Peer Pressure: Standing Firm in Faith

Peer pressure is like a strong wind that tries to push you in a direction you might not want to go. It can come in many forms, from subtle suggestions to outright challenges, and can affect your choices about what you wear, what you say, and even what you believe. Imagine yourself in the lunchroom, watching your friends make arrangements to skip class. You feel a tug inside, a conflict between fitting in and staying true to your values. This isn't just about skipping a class; it's about defining who you are and what you stand for. Peer pressure challenges your commitment to uphold your values, and it can be difficult to stay strong when you feel isolated.

The story of Daniel is a powerful biblical example of resisting peer pressure. When Babylon took Daniel captive, they pressured him to eat the king's food, which would have violated his dietary restrictions and his commitment to God. Instead of yielding to this pressure, Daniel proposed a test: he and his friends would eat only vegetables and water for ten days. The result? They ended up healthier than those who ate the king's rich food. Daniel's story isn't just about food; it's about a young man who stood firm in his faith, even in a foreign land, under the pressure to conform. His courage to remain faithful to his beliefs in the face of adversity provides a blueprint for us to follow.

If you ever encounter peer pressure, consider Daniel and adopt practical strategies to stay strong in your faith. Begin with assertive communication.

Assertiveness doesn't mean being aggressive or confrontational but confidently expressing your beliefs and boundaries. For example, a simple but firm **"No, thanks, that's not for me"** can be powerful if someone tries to persuade you to do something you're uncomfortable with. It communicates your stance in a respectful yet unyielding way.

Role-playing can be an effective way to prepare for these situations. Try this with a trusted friend or family member: have them act out different scenarios where you might face peer pressure. Practice responding in ways that are both assertive and true to your beliefs. This exercise can build confidence and help you feel more prepared when real-life situations arise. It's like a rehearsal for your values, ensuring you're ready to perform when the curtain of peer pressure rises.

Lastly, always appreciate the role of the Holy Spirit in helping you resist peer pressure. As a believer, you can access a profound source of strength and wisdom beyond your capabilities. When you feel overwhelmed or uncertain, take a moment to pray, asking the Holy Spirit to give you the courage and clarity you need to make the right choices. **The Holy Spirit is a constant helper**, ready to guide you through every challenge, providing peace and assurance when required.

Dealing with peer pressure requires more than just saying no. It's also about understanding why you are saying no. The key is to avoid negative influences and actively pursue a path that aligns with your faith and values. As you face these challenges, remember that you are not alone. With biblical examples, practical tools, and divine support, you can resist conformity and flourish as a beacon of God's truth and love in your world.

2.3 COMMUNICATING WITH PARENTS: BRIDGING THE GENERATION GAP

Navigating conversations with your parents can sometimes feel like trying to decode a foreign language. It's not just about the difference in slang or preferences in music; it's about bridging a gap in perspectives that comes from growing up in different eras.

Understanding these generational differences is critical to fostering **empathy and respect** in family relationships. Just like you, the world your parents were raised in influenced their perspectives, values, and fears. They may place a high value on security, having been raised during economic uncertainty. At the same time, you might prioritize passion and purpose, growing up in an age rich with opportunities. Acknowledging these differences doesn't mean you have to agree on everything, but it can help you see where they're coming from, making conversations less about winning and more about understanding.

Clarity and respect are your best tools when it comes to expressing yourself. Whether you're discussing your weekend plans or a new career aspiration, the way you communicate can open doors or build walls. Start by being clear about your thoughts and feelings. It's easy to assume that your parents know what you mean, but clarity prevents misunderstandings. For instance, if you feel overwhelmed by expectations, instead of saying, "You don't understand me," try explaining, **"I feel stressed when it seems like my efforts go unnoticed, and I need us to discuss my schedule."** This approach shows your perspective without putting them on the defensive.

Remember, it's not just about what you say but **how you say it**. Approaching the conversation respectfully and openly sets a tone that encourages them to listen and respond kindly.

Reflecting on the Fifth Commandment, **"Honor your father and your mother,"** offers a deeper insight into the value God places on family relationships. This command isn't about obedience without question; it's about respecting your parents' role in your life, recognizing their sacrifices, and valuing their desire to see you succeed. In modern terms, honoring your parents is about treating them with fundamental respect, even when you disagree. It's about acknowledging their position without forfeiting your voice. Balancing this respect with your growing independence is a delicate dance, but it's possible with open, honest communication.

Establishing regular check-ins with your parents can turn obligatory updates into **meaningful exchanges.** These check-ins can be as formal or informal as you like, over a weekly family dinner or a coffee on Sunday afternoons. Use this time to share about your life—your successes, your worries, and your day-to-day experiences. Invite them to share, too. This practice keeps the lines of communication open and builds a foundation of trust and mutual respect. Over time, these talks can ease misunderstandings and create an opportunity to navigate the challenging aspects of your relationship.

As you engage in these dialogues, you'll likely discover more about your parents—as your guardians and individuals with their hopes and fears. This understanding can enrich your relationship, providing a more profound sense of connection and mutual respect. It's about taking steps toward each other, bridging the gap one conversation at a time, and fostering a family dynamic that thrives on understanding and mutual respect. Whether it's planning your future or choosing what to do on a Friday night, these conversations are the threads that, when woven together, form the rich tapestry of your family life.

2.4 CONFLICT RESOLUTION: FOLLOWING JESUS' FOOTSTEPS

Imagine you're in a situation where a close friend says something that hurts you deeply. The sting of their words might make you want to pull away or lash out in anger. But what if you chose a path of understanding and reconciliation instead? This approach concerns making peace and following Jesus' teachings on resolving conflicts.

In Matthew 18:15-17, Jesus provides clear steps for addressing disputes: "*If your brother or sister sins, go and point out their fault, just between the two of you. If they listen to you, you have won them over. But if they will not listen, take one or two others along so that 'every matter may be established by the testimony of two or three witnesses. If they still refuse to listen, tell it to the church, and if they refuse to listen even to the church, treat them as you would a pagan or a tax collector." Jesus emphasizes the importance of direct communication and handling conflicts with care and honesty.*"

In the parable of the unforgiving servant (Matthew 18:21-35), Jesus reminds us how to treat others about forgiveness. The story starts with Peter asking Jesus, "Lord, how many times shall I forgive my brother or sister who sins against me? Up to seven times?" Jesus replies, **"I tell you, not seven times, but seventy-seven times"** (Matthew 18:21-22), highlighting that forgiveness should be limitless. In the parable, a servant is forgiven a massive debt by his master, who then harshly demands a small debt from another servant. When the master learns of this, he rebukes the servant, saying, **"Shouldn't you have had mercy on your fellow servant just as I had on you?"** (Matthew 18:33). The master punishes the unforgiving servant for not showing the same mercy he received. This story teaches us a vital lesson: God calls us to forgive as He forgives us. Holding onto grudges or resentment harms our relationships and burdens our hearts. While forgiveness isn't always easy, it is vital to finding **peace and healing.**

One of the most effective ways to resolve conflicts is through **active listening**. Active listening is one of the most effective ways to resolve disputes. It involves focusing, understanding, responding, and remembering what is said. It's more than just hearing words; it shows the other person that their feelings and thoughts are essential to you. Instead of thinking about what you'll say next, try to understand where they are coming from. Another helpful approach is using **"I" statements**. For example, instead of saying, "You never listen to me," try saying, "I feel unheard when I talk about my day, and the conversation quickly shifts." This way of expressing yourself conveys your feelings without blaming the other person, which can help prevent conflict from escalating.

Sometimes, conflicts are more challenging to resolve on your own, and that's okay. If your efforts to reconcile aren't working, consider seeking mediation. Choosing mediation isn't about admitting defeat; it's about recognizing when additional support is needed to find a resolution. Trusted friends, family members, or counselors can serve as mediators, providing an impartial perspective and facilitating a constructive conversation. They can help clarify misunderstandings and guide both parties toward a solution that works for everyone.

Being a peacemaker isn't just a task; it's a calling for Christians. It reflects the peace of Christ, who reconciled us to God through His sacrifice. As peacemakers, we play an active role in God's work by bringing harmony where there's discord and understanding where there's confusion. This role extends beyond our relationships; it influences our communities and the world. To foster an environment where peace can thrive, consider setting up a peer mediation program at your school or organizing community dialogues on pressing local issues. By taking these steps, you're not just resolving conflicts but also helping to build a culture of peace and mutual respect.

Adopting these principles and practices for resolving conflicts can transform how you handle disputes and disagreements. It encourages you to move from a mindset focused on division to one centered on forgiveness and healing. It's about viewing conflict not as a problem to avoid but as an opportunity for growth and deeper understanding. As you navigate the ups and downs of relationships, remember that each conflict offers a chance to demonstrate the love and peace of Christ. You have the tools to resolve disputes and create more robust, resilient bonds with those around you.

2.5 BUILDING TRUST: THE CORNERSTONE OF CHRISTIAN RELATIONSHIPS

Trust isn't just a word—it's the glue that holds our relationships together, giving them strength and resilience. In Christian relationships, trust becomes even more profound. It's rooted in biblical principles like those found in Proverbs 3:5- 6, which advises, **"Trust in the Lord with all your heart and lean**

not on your understanding." While this scripture speaks to our relationship with God, it also extends to how we interact with others. Just as we trust God completely, we should strive to build relationships where trust is a foundation, reflecting God's faithfulness in our actions.

Building Trust: Small Steps, Big Impact

Building trust takes time and involves small, consistent actions. Think of it like planting a flower in a garden. You water it, give it sunlight, and, with patience, it begins to bloom. Trust is like that—it's strengthened by showing up for your friends, keeping your promises, and being there when they need you.

Here's an example: Imagine you promised your friend you'd help them study for a test. Even when it's inconvenient, keeping that promise is like watering that flower—you're helping trust grow between you. These small actions may seem simple, but they build strong and lasting friendships.

What Happens When Trust is Broken?

But what do you do when someone breaks your trust? It can feel like a storm has knocked over a tree in your garden, causing damage and leaving everything looking a bit broken. But remember, a fallen tree doesn't mean the garden is ruined. In the same way, broken trust doesn't mean a relationship is over.

Rebuilding trust is a journey that begins with facing the issue head-on with honesty. This honesty serves as a compass, guiding us through rebuilding what was lost.

Rebuilding trust involves:

- Openly conversing about what happened.

- Acknowledging the hurt.

- Genuinely committing to make things right.

It's like planting a new tree—it takes time and effort, but with care, trust can grow back stronger than before.

Practical Tips for Building Trust

1. **Be Honest and Transparent**: Being truthful about your thoughts and feelings, even when uncomfortable, helps create an environment where trust can thrive. Think of honesty as the sunlight and water that trust needs to grow.

2. **Avoid Gossip**: Gossip destroys trust as quickly as it is built. To build trust, focus on speaking directly and avoid talking behind people's backs. Instead, focus on lifting others and being a positive force in your friend group.

3. **Keep Your Promises**: Do it if you say you will do something. It shows reliability and helps others feel secure in their relationship with you.

4. **Ask for Forgiveness and Offer It**: When trust is broken, be willing to apologize and make amends. Also, be ready to forgive when someone comes to you with a sincere apology. Remember, forgiveness is a vital part of building a solid relationship.

Reflect on Trust in Your Relationships

Reflect on Trust in Your Relationships: Take a moment to think about the friendships in your life. Can you identify areas where you could strengthen trust? You may need to apologize for something or be more consistent in keeping your promises. There may be friends you need to set boundaries with because their actions have broken trust in the past. This reflection is a mirror that can help you see where trust needs to be nurtured in your relationships.

Use these reflection questions in your journal to guide you:

- **What small steps can I take to build trust with my friends and family?**

- **Is there someone I need to forgive or ask for forgiveness from?**

- **How can I be more honest and transparent in my relationships?**

Trust in the Bigger Picture

Trust impacts individual relationships and entire communities. In a youth group or church setting, trust helps create a supportive and cohesive environment where everyone feels safe to express themselves, share their struggles, and grow in faith.

Leaders and members alike have a role in fostering this trust. Everyone contributes to a community that reflects God's love and trustworthiness by being open, honest, and dependable. When trust grows within a group, so does its ability to positively impact both within the group and in the broader world.

Conclusion: Growing Together in Trust

Building trust is like nurturing a garden. It takes time, effort, and care, but the results are beautiful and worth it. Remember that trust is foundational as you continue to grow in your relationships. It's what makes friendships strong and communities vibrant. Whether rebuilding trust after a storm or nurturing it daily, know that you are cultivating something precious and lasting. Trust enriches your relationships and strengthens your walk with God, helping you grow into who He created you to be.

2.6 Saying No with Love: Setting Boundaries in Friendships

Imagine your life as a beautiful garden that you nurture with the best intentions, ensuring every element within it helps it flourish. Just as weeding is essential for a garden's health, setting boundaries is crucial for maintaining healthy, long-lasting friendships. Boundaries help define what is okay and what is not, allowing you to honor your values and needs while respecting those of others. They are essential because they protect your emotional energy, prevent resentment, and enhance the quality of your relationships.

So, how do you establish and communicate these boundaries? It starts with understanding yourself and recognizing your limits. What are you comfortable with? What are your core values? Reflecting on these questions helps you identify where you need to set boundaries. For example, if you value quiet time in the evening, you might set a boundary by not accepting phone calls after a particular hour. Communicating these boundaries clearly and assertively is critical. **It's not about being harsh but being honest and direct.**

You might say, "I love our chats, but I don't take calls after 9 PM so I can unwind before bed. Can we talk tomorrow earlier in the day?" This approach shows you respect your needs and the other person's time.

But what happens when someone doesn't respect your boundaries? It can be challenging, especially if it's someone you care about. First, reinforce your boundaries with clarity. Remind them of what you previously agreed upon and express how important it is for you. If the behavior continues, it may be necessary to increase the distance in the relationship, at least temporarily. The focus here is on safeguarding your well-being, not on punishment. It's okay to say, "I need some space right now," and spend your energy where it's respected and reciprocated.

In biblical teachings, Jesus himself showed us the importance of setting boundaries. His directive in Matthew 5:37, **"Let your 'yes' be 'yes,' and your 'no' be 'no,"** underscores the importance of being transparent and honest in our interactions. This teaching does not just apply to keeping promises but also to how we communicate our limits to others. Being upfront with our responses, saying yes or no, shows integrity and respect for ourselves and those nearby. Jesus knew the importance of boundaries even in His ministry. He took time away from the crowds to pray or rest, showing that taking care of oneself is not selfish but necessary for serving others effectively.

Establishing and maintaining boundaries is not a one-time task but an ongoing process that requires attention and adjustment as relationships grow and change. It's about nurturing your personal space and understanding when to invite others and when to prioritize yourself.

As we wrap up this chapter, remember that establishing boundaries is a way to show self-respect and care for yourself and your friends. The key is to have relationships that support and contribute to your growth and happiness rather than impede it. From choosing friends wisely to communicating effectively with parents to handling conflicts and building trust, each step in this chapter equips you to navigate the complexities of relationships with grace and confidence.

ACTIVITY - CHAPTER 2

Scan the QR code.

Give Us Your
Feedback!

How Do You Like Our Book So Far?

We'd love to hear your thoughts! Take a quick break to leave a review by scanning the QR code or click the link below. Your feedback can inspire other young girls on their journey.

THANK YOU!

Chapter 3

Managing Anxiety and Stress Through Faith

Amid your busy day, it can feel like a challenge to find moments of calm, like finding a quiet spot in a crowded city. It's easy to let the weight of expectations, deadlines, and social pressures pile up until you feel like you're carrying a backpack filled with bricks. But what if you could find a sanctuary where you can lay down your burdens and experience renewal? This sanctuary isn't a physical place but a spiritual refuge you can access through prayer.

This chapter explores the power of prayer as a stress reliever, offering temporary relief and long-lasting peace.

3.1 FINDING PEACE IN PRAYER: SIMPLE TECHNIQUES FOR STRESSFUL TIMES

View prayer as a personal chat room with God, where the connection is constant, and the line is always open. It's a space where you can be wholly yourself—no pretenses, no filters, just you and God, heart to heart. In this sacred space, you can pour out all your worries, deepest fears, and moments of joy and gratitude. The beauty of prayer is that it requires no special equipment or specific location. You can reach out to God at your desk, on a bus, or in bed at night. And the best part? He's always ready to listen.

To deepen your prayer life, incorporate structured prayer techniques such as **the ACTS method: Adoration, Confession, Thanksgiving, and Supplication.**

This method provides a simple framework that can help guide your prayers, making them more focused and comprehensive. Begin with the step of Adoration, where you praise God for His love, mercy, and omnipotence, setting a tone of reverence and worship. Then, move on to Confession, where you openly acknowledge your regrets and mistakes, seeking His forgiveness. This step is cleansing, allowing you to let go of guilt and receive God's grace. Then comes Thanksgiving, expressing gratitude for your life's big and small blessings, which can shift your perspective from what you lack to the abundance you possess. Finally, Supplication is when you bring your requests to God, asking for His help, guidance, and intervention in specific areas of your life.

However, don't reserve prayer just for times of intense stress. Consider setting specific times for prayer—maybe in the morning to set the tone for your day, a quick midday check-in, and a reflective moment before bed. These regular contact points can give your soul a break, helping you stay calm and focused during the chaos.

Now, let's talk about the real-life impact of prayer through stories from teens like you who have found solace and strength in their prayer lives. Emily, a 16-year-old from Texas, shares, "Last year, I was stressed about my exams. I felt like I was drowning in study notes and practice tests.

Starting my day with prayer helped me keep my anxiety in check. It reminded me that God was with me; I wasn't alone. And you know what? Not only did I do well on my exams, but I also felt more at peace throughout the whole process."

Then there's Jordan, who started praying for ten minutes every night before going to sleep: "It became something I looked forward to each day.

Pouring out my worries and thanking God for the good in my life made me feel lighter and more optimistic. My prayer time reset my mindset and helped me handle things better."

Reflective Exercise: Prayer Journaling

To make your prayer practice more engaging, try keeping a prayer journal. You received a bonus activity in this book to help you create your own prayer journal, but if you prefer, many faith-centered journals offer prompts and scriptural quotes to guide your reflections.

When I started journaling as a teen, I found one at Sam's Club; the prompts in Sam's journal helped me focus and drew me into the practice. Use a simple notebook to write down your prayers, thoughts, and any responses you feel you're receiving from God. Not only does this help in organizing your thoughts, but it also provides a physical record of your spiritual journey. Over time, you can see how God has moved in your life, answered prayers, and helped you grow. Writing can be a form of meditation, allowing you to slow down and strengthen your connection to your faith.

Embracing prayer as your refuge can transform the way you handle stress and anxiety. It's not about escaping reality but about enriching your reality with spiritual strength and peace. As you continue to explore and expand your prayer life, remember that this isn't about perfection. It's about persistence. The more you turn to prayer, the more natural it will become, and the deeper your peace will grow. So, next time you feel overwhelmed, remember that your sanctuary is just a prayer away.

3.2 Anxious for Nothing: Biblical Promises for Mental Wellness

In those quiet moments when the world seems too much, and our hearts feel too heavy, God whispers promises of peace and presence through His Word. Scriptures are not just ancient texts; they are living words that breathe life into our weary souls, especially when anxiety tries to grip our hearts. Let's explore critical verses that serve as anchors in turbulent times, offering reassurance of God's unwavering support and love.

Philippians 4:6-7 tells us, **"Do not be anxious about anything, but in every situation, by prayer and petition, with Thanksgiving, present your requests to God. And the peace of God, which transcends all understanding, will guard your hearts and minds in Christ Jesus."** Here, Paul isn't just suggesting that we shouldn't worry; he's providing a divine strategy to combat anxiety. The key is to turn our focus from fear to God through prayer and embracing gratitude in our requests. This shift doesn't just change our immediate feelings; it transforms our overall mindset, reinforcing our mental wellness with the peace of God—a peace so profound it surpasses all understanding.

Similarly, 1 Peter 5:7 encourages us **"to Cast all your anxiety on Him because He cares for you."** This verse is a gentle reminder that we are not burdening God with our worries; instead, we are placing them in the hands of someone capable of handling them. It highlights God's concern for us, assuring us that our worries are significant to Him.

Applying these scriptures to your daily life can be transformative. When anxiety looms, recall these verses. Speak them out loud or quietly in your heart. They should be your first thought in the morning and your last before sleep. This practice isn't about denying stressors but about fortifying your heart and mind with the truth of God's Word, ensuring that your reactions to anxiety are grounded in **faith, not fear**.

To help internalize these truths:

1. Start a Scripture memory plan.

2. Dedicate a few minutes each day to memorize one anxiety-relieving Scripture each week.

3. Write them on index cards, set them as reminders on your phone, or stick them on your mirror.

This practice is more than rote memorization; it's about weaving God's promises into the fabric of your being, strengthening your spiritual armor so that when anxiety strikes, you're ready to counter it with the truth.

In moments of overwhelming stress, take inspiration from David, a man after God's heart who frequently deals with anxiety and fear. Despite his hardships—from facing Goliath as a young shepherd to evading King Saul's jealous wrath—David consistently turned to God, expressing all his emotions through the Psalms.

Through his candid conversations with God, he teaches us that we don't need to conceal or repress our feelings of anxiety. Instead, they can be channels for a more profound connection with God. For instance, in Psalm 56:3, David writes, **"When I am afraid, I put my trust in you."** His words reveal a fundamental truth: acknowledging our fear is the first step towards overcoming it through faith. David's reliance on God during his trials provides a powerful blueprint: when anxiety arises, turn to God, trusting that He is our refuge and strength, an ever-present help in trouble (Psalm 46:1).

When you internalize these scriptures and draw inspiration from biblical figures like David, you prepare yourself with spiritual tools to navigate the challenges of anxiety. Remember, God's Word is alive and active, sharper than any two-edged sword—it cuts through our fears and reassures us of His eternal, unchangeable love and support. As you continue to build your spiritual defenses through Scripture and prayer, you create a stronghold of peace in your heart, one that stands firm against the waves of anxiety and stress. Hold onto these truths and witness how they change anxiety into peace, trial into testimony, and fear into faith.

3.3 MINDFULNESS AND MEDITATION: CHRISTIAN APPROACHES TO CALM

Finding peace in our fast-paced world can be challenging. Christian mindfulness and meditation offer a way to help calm the mind and connect spiritually. Rooted in biblical tradition, they provide spiritual grounding to help you navigate the chaos of everyday life with peace and purpose.

Mindfulness in a Christian context isn't about emptying your mind or aligning with Eastern spiritual practices; instead, it's about filling your mind with God's presence and aligning your thoughts with His peace. It involves being fully present in the moment, being aware of your surroundings, and being open to God's voice. Meditation extends this by focusing intensely on God's Word or attributes, allowing His truths to soak into your heart and transform your mind. Think of it as contemplating a Scripture verse, not just reading it but letting it read you, exploring every nuance, and applying its truths to your life.

An effective technique for Christian meditation involves concentrating on a particular verse of Scripture. Start by selecting a verse that speaks to your current needs or challenges. For example, Philippians 4:6-7 is a comforting choice if you're anxious. Take your time and read the verse slowly, paying attention to every word and phrase and repeating them multiple times. As you meditate, ask yourself what this verse says about God's character, promises, and commands. Consider how it applies to your specific situation. This process accomplishes two critical things: it deepens your understanding of the Scripture and embeds it in your heart, resulting in a stronger faith and enhanced spiritual clarity.

Nature can also be a powerful aid in Christian-focused mindfulness. Spending time in God's creation can help you see His majesty and care in the details of the natural world. Whether it's a walk in the park, a moment by a lake, or just sitting under a tree in your backyard, nature provides a backdrop to help you focus on God and His provisions. During these moments, focus on fully present by observing the beauty around you and expressing gratitude to God for His creation. Practicing this mindfulness relieves stress and deepens your appreciation for the Creator.

Prayer walks are another dynamic way to engage in mindfulness. These can be as simple as walking through your neighborhood while praying silently. Present your thoughts, concerns, and praises to God in each step. Use walking as a metaphor for moving forward in your faith journey, letting go of burdens, and receiving strength from God. This active form of meditation can be beneficial if you find it challenging to sit still and focus. It combines physical activity with spiritual practice, enriching your body and soul.

The benefits of these practices are profound. Regular mindfulness and meditation practice can significantly reduce stress, as they help you focus on the stability and peace that God provides. They also improve concentration, helping you stay present and engaged in daily tasks and interactions. Perhaps most importantly, they can deepen your relationship with God as you spend intentional time in His presence, listening for His voice and aligning your spirit with His.

Practical Exercise: Five-Minute Biblical Meditation

Let's try a simple exercise to get you started. Choose a quiet place where you won't be disturbed. Sit comfortably and close your eyes. Breathe deeply for a few moments, letting your body relax. Now, think of a verse that you find comforting, such as Matthew 11:28, **"Come to me, all you who are weary and burdened, and I will give you rest."** Repeat this verse silently, focusing on each word. With each inhale, imagine drawing in God's peace. With each exhale, picture releasing your worries and tensions. Continue this for five minutes. When you finish, take a moment to reflect on how you feel. You might notice a sense of calmness, a deeper connection with God, or a renewed perspective on your challenges.

As you practice these techniques, you'll find that you're better equipped to handle the pressures of life and cultivate a deeper, more meaningful relationship with God. Explore these practices and watch how they enrich your spiritual life and everyday experiences.

3.4 UNPLUGGING TO UNWIND: MANAGING DIGITAL STRESSORS

Our phones often feel part of our bodies, making it challenging to acknowledge our dependence on the digital realm. We may not be aware of it, but our stress levels can skyrocket because of constant notifications, social media updates, and the compulsion to check messages. This digital overload can make you feel you're on a never-ending treadmill of scrolling and responding, which is exhausting. The good news? Implementing a digital detox—even a short one—can help you reclaim your calm and significantly reduce your anxiety.

First things first, let's talk about what a digital detox involves. It's not about throwing your phone into a lake (tempting as that might sound sometimes!). It's all about giving your mind a break by intentionally taking breaks from digital devices. Start small by establishing specific no-phone hours each day. For example, you might designate dinner or the hour before bed as tech-free periods. Establishing these tech-free times helps create a routine that your mind and body come to expect, gradually reducing your dependence on digital devices. Setting up tech-free zones within your home is another effective strategy. Make your bedroom a phone-free area, which can help improve your sleep quality and give you a peaceful space to relax without distractions.

What should you do when you are usually on your phone or computer? It is an opportunity to rediscover activities that enrich your life offline. **Engaging in physical activities is a fantastic start.**

Whether it's yoga, swing, or just a walk in the park, moving your body is good for your physical health and a great way to clear your mind. If you're not in your thoughts, how about losing yourself in a good book or exploring creative outlets like painting or writing? These therapeutic activities allow you to express yourself and unwind without digital interference.

Let's hear real-life stories from teens who've successfully navigated the path of digital detox. Take Sarah, a high school junior who cut down her social media use. She started by deleting her social media apps every weekend. Initially, she worried she might miss out on what her friends were doing, but she found herself more present in her own life. She spent more time with her family, rediscovered her love for sketching, and felt less stressed and more content with her daily life.

Then there's Mark, who placed his evening gaming with reading and occasionally astronomy through his telescope. He shares, "The first few" nights were tough. I missed my gaming sessions. But then I started looking forward to my reading time. It's like I first how much I enjoyed getting lost in stories. Plus, stargazing is just incredible. It makes my problems seem smaller when I look at the stars.

These stories" s highlight the positive changes that can come from stepping back from our screens. It's not about letting out technology entirely but about finding a healthier balance that allows you to enjoy the best of both worlds. As you experiment with these strategies, notice the changes in how you feel. More relaxed? Less anxious? More connected to the people and activities that truly matter? These are the real signs that you're successful in managing the digital noise that modern life throws at us. Keep exploring what works best for you, and remember, every step back from the screen is a step toward a more balanced, peaceful life.

3.5 JOURNALING FOR JESUS: REFLECTIVE PRACTICES FOR ANXIETY RELIEF

Imagine owning a special notebook resembling a best friend—always there to listen without judgment and help make sense of your world. You can find that in spiritual journaling. It's Where you can express every thought, detail your day, pour out your worries, and celebrate your joys. Think of it as a sanctuary where you can delve into your inner world without interruptions or concerns about others' opinions. Practice isn't just about writing what happened during your day; it's a reflection exercise where you can connect your experiences to your faith, discover deeper feelings, and consider how God is moving in your life.

Remember, your journal is a tool to deepen your relationship with God. Use it to pour out your heart, document your prayers, and reflect on scripture. Over time, you'll find it becomes a valuable record of your spiritual journey, showing how God has guided you, answered your prayers, and helped you grow in faith. Embrace this practice with an open heart and see how it transforms your daily walk with God.

Once you have your journal, decide on a regular writing schedule. It doesn't have to be daily. The key is consistency. Establish a journaling habit by dedicating the same time each day or week. Early mornings might work for you, or reflecting before bed helps you unwind. Whenever you choose, make sure it's a time when you can be calm and undisturbed.

What to write about can vary. Consider starting with daily gratitudes and making a list of things you're grateful for each day. Gratitude journaling helps you focus on the abundance in your life rather than what's lacking, fostering a sense of contentment and joy. You can strengthen your faith by writing prayer requests detailing concerns for yourself and others and tracking how these prayers are answered. This habit also provides tangible reminders of God's presence.

Personal reflections on Scripture can also be enriching. Write about how certain verses resonate with you or how biblical stories parallel your experiences. This practice deepens your understanding of the Bible and its relevance to everyday life.

There is ample evidence supporting the therapeutic benefits of journaling. It provides a way to process complex emotions and can lead to significant reductions in anxiety and stress. When you write about your worries, you transfer them from your mind to paper, making them seem smaller and more manageable. This process helps declutter your mind, allowing you to think more clearly and sleep better. Journaling also offers a unique way to track your personal growth. When you reflect on previous experiences, you can witness how obstacles that appeared impossible to overcome are now evidence of your strength and the grace of God.

Creative Journaling Ideas

Consider incorporating art, poetry, or music elements to bring more vibrancy to your journaling. These creative expressions can enhance connecting with God and processing your feelings. If you love drawing, sketch something representing a pivotal moment of your day or how a particular Bible verse makes you feel. Poetry can be a powerful tool to condense complex emotions into a few poignant lines, helping you capture the essence of your thoughts. You might even create a playlist of songs that speak to your soul, noting in your journal how these tunes uplift you or bring you peace.

Adding these creative elements to your journal can bring a new depth and dynamism to your reflections. They allow you to engage different parts of your brain, making the journaling experience more engaging and fulfilling. Through exploring other forms of expression, your journal transforms into a vibrant canvas that depicts your spiritual journey, growth, learning, and finding peace in God's presence.

3.6 SLEEP IN PEACE: BIBLICAL TIPS FOR RESTFUL NIGHTS

Picture yourself climbing into bed after a tiring day, enjoying the cozy sheets, and peacefully falling asleep, recharging your energy. It sounds lovely. Many people toss and turn at night, consumed by worries. But what if the Bible's wisdom holds the secrets to a restful night?

Scriptures like Psalm 4:8, **"In peace, I will lie down and sleep, for you alone, Lord, make me dwell in safety,"** remind us that" God is not only a refuge from the chaos of the day but also a provider of profound peace that can lead to restful sleep. Similarly, Matthew 11:28-30 invites us to come to Jesus when we are weary and burdened, promising rest for our souls. These verses aren't just parenting words but invitations to trust God with our nights and days.

Consider including a simple prayer in your nightly routine to reinforce this trust and cultivate a peaceful mindset before bed. You might pray:

"Dear Heavenly Father, please give my mind peace and take the worries of tomorrow away from me, for I know that all is in Your hands and Your will be done. With this knowledge, please help me to rest. In Jesus' name, Amen"

Incorporating this prayer can help foster a sense of calm and remind you to release your anxieties to God, trusting in His care and guidance.

Establishing a bedtime routine is crucial for turning these promises into your nightly reality. A consistent routine signals your body that it's time to go down and prepare for sleep. Start by setting a bedtime and sticking to it as much as possible, even on weekends. About an hour before this, begin your wind-down process: turn off electronic devices, as the blue light emitted can disrupt your natural sleep cycle. Instead, you might read a book, write in your journal, or do some light stretching—activities that don't just donate time but soothe your mind and prepare your heart for restful sleep.

Creating a restful environment also plays a crucial role in enhancing your sleep quality. Transform your bedroom into a sleep sanctuary by customizing lighting, temperature, and noise levels for optimal comfort. Little touches like scented candles or essential oils with lavender or chamomile can also add to the calming atmosphere, making your bedroom a cue for relaxation and sleep.

Most importantly, learn to trust God for peaceful sleep. Before you go to bed, spend a few minutes in prayer, casting every care and worry onto Him, as 1 Peter 5:7 advises. Handing your worries to God can be incredibly freeing, allowing you to rest assured of His care and presence. It's about letting go of the day's burdens and trusting that God holds you, your worries, and your dreams in His hands.

You can invite God's peace into your evenings by incorporating these biblical insights and practical tips into your nightly routine. Sleep is no longer simply a requirement but a nightly act of faith and trust that renews both body and spirit. As you lay down each night, remember that God is with you, guarding your sleep and renewing you for the days ahead, just as He promises in His Word.

As we come to the end of this chapter on managing anxiety and stress through faith, keep in mind that each strategy we've covered is not only for coping but also for thriving. These practices ground you in God's peace and empower you to face each day with renewed strength and calm. As you apply these principles, watch how they transform your nights and days, empowering you to live a life marked by spiritual peace and resilience.

ACTIVITY - CHAPTER 3

Scan the QR code

Chapter 4

Cultivating a Deep and Personal Faith

Imagine yourself embarking on a journey through a lush, vibrant forest. **Each step symbolizes a day in your life, and the path represents your faith journey.**

Some days, the path is clear and bright, filled with sunshine, and easy to navigate. On other days, the path might be foggy, and the terrain could become challenging, making it hard to see clearly or feel stable. In these moments, cultivating a deep and personal faith becomes essential—just like tending to a difficult trail—ensuring you have the strength and guidance to navigate whatever comes your way. It equips you with the necessary tools and determination to face any weather conditions confidently. And as you overcome these challenges, you'll feel a sense of accomplishment that will fuel your journey further.

Now, let's put on our boots and begin this chapter by examining how daily devotions can resemble essential trail markers, and rest stops that guide and support you on your journey.

4.1 DAILY DEVOTIONS: MAKING TIME FOR GOD AMIDST SCHOOL AND SOCIAL LIFE

Finding time for daily devotions can be challenging with school assignments, extracurricular activities, and social commitments. However, like taking a quick pause in a calm location, spending time in God's presence can also empower and revitalize your soul. Daily devotions aren't just another task on your to-do list; they are spiritual nourishment that fortifies your faith, offers divine guidance, and aligns your daily walk with God's purposes.

Creating a habit of daily devotions starts with recognizing their value. Just as you wouldn't go a day without eating because you need physical nourishment, skipping spiritual nourishment can leave you feeling weak and directionless. These moments with God are your spiritual meals, the sustenance that strengthens your faith's roots deep into the soil of God's truth, making you steadfast in life's storms. They provide wisdom for your decisions, comfort in your troubles, and joy in your achievements, anchoring you in God's unchanging love. More than that, they align your daily walk with God's purposes, giving you a sense of guidance and purpose in your life.

While it may appear overwhelming, some planning can make devotion to your busy schedule more manageable. Think about moments in your day that naturally align with your routine. For many people, mornings are great for setting a positive tone for the day.

Consider waking up a few minutes earlier to read a devotional passage and pray before the day gets busy. If mornings are too rushed, how about making your devotion time part of your wind-down routine at night? Reflecting on a Scripture verse or a devotional reading can be a peaceful way to end your day, filling your thoughts with God's peace instead of the day's stresses.

Maintain this habit by setting up a peaceful and inviting space for personal reflection. You don't need an elaborate setup—just a cozy corner of your room with a comfortable chair, a small table for your Bible and journal, and perhaps a lamp for soft lighting can create the perfect environment.

Personalize this space with items that inspire you, like inspirational quotes, a cross, or even a houseplant—anything that reminds you of God's presence and helps you shift from the hustle and bustle to a state of reflection and peace. You can also include items that hold personal significance, such as a family heirloom or a piece of art that resonates with your faith. These personal touches can make your devotional space more meaningful and conducive to spiritual reflection.

Maintaining motivation for daily devotions can be challenging, but you don't have to do it alone. Partnering with a friend or a mentor to share what you've learned and discuss your insights can enrich your experience. This accountability can keep you both committed to your devotional time and turn what might sometimes feel like a solo trek into an encouraging partnership in faith. You can engage in devotional readings, pray for one another, and celebrate God's work, creating a shared adventure of faith with mutual support and understanding. Having someone to share your journey with can provide additional perspectives, encouragement, and accountability, making your faith journey more fulfilling and rewarding.

By weaving daily devotions into the fabric of your life, you create a rhythm of spiritual intimacy with God that carries you through each day with purpose and peace. Whether dealing with school challenges, life decisions, or daily pressures, connecting with God is your spiritual lifeline, keeping you anchored and aligned with His will. So, grab that journal, find that perfect spot, and make these daily devotions a highlight of your day—not just a habit but a heartfelt rendezvous with your Creator.

4.2 SCRIPTURE MEMORIZATION: HIDING GOD'S WORD IN YOUR HEART

Have you ever had a song stuck in your head and hummed throughout the day? Just imagine if the words of that song were meaningful Scripture verses, offering you strength, comfort, and guidance precisely when you need them. This is the power of scripture memorization. It's like having a playlist of divine truths at your fingertips, ready to be accessed whenever and wherever, whether during a demanding test or a complicated relationship. Embedding God's Word in your heart is not only a shield against temptation but a wellspring of wisdom and a constant source of comfort during times of distress. It's like having a trusted friend who is always there for you, providing immediate reassurance and support.

Memorizing Scripture sounds daunting at first. But it's something anyone can achieve, and the benefits are profound. By memorizing verses, you provide the Holy Spirit with internal tools to guide and comfort you.

For instance, when feelings of inadequacy or anxiety creep in, recalling a verse like Philippians 4:13, **"I can do all things through Christ who strengthens me,"** can provide an immediate source of encouragement and strength. Or when you're tempted to follow the crowd in a way that conflicts with your values, remember 1 Corinthians 10:13—**"No temptation has come your way that is beyond what others have faced. God is faithful; He will not let you be tempted beyond your ability to resist. Instead, He will provide a way out with every temptation so you can endure it."** These aren't just words, promises, and truths that can actively shape and direct your life.

Here are a few techniques to make scripture memorization more accessible and practical. First, repetition is your friend. Just like learning the lyrics to a new song, repeating a verse several times throughout the day helps cement it in your memory. You can say it out loud, write it down, or even sing it—whatever works best for you. Another helpful method is using note cards. Write the verse on one side; on the other, write the reference. Carry these cards with you, or place them where you'll see them regularly, like on your bathroom mirror or your car's dashboard. This visibility keeps the verses in your daily visual landscape, reinforcing your memorization efforts.

An effective way to anchor verses in your routine is by associating them with daily tasks. For example, while brushing your teeth, you could focus on a verse about purification like Psalm 51:10, **"Create in me a clean heart, O God, and renew a right spirit within me."** Or, while packing your school bag, consider Ephesians 6:11 about putting on the armor of God. These associations tie Scripture to the rhythm of your daily life, making memorization more practical and relevant.

Incorporating music or rhythm into your memorization can also enhance your recall of verses. Many find that setting Scripture to a simple tune or beat helps lock it into memory. Find songs directly based on Scripture and add them to your playlist to reinforce the verses each time you listen.

Consider starting a 30-day scripture memorization challenge to give you a structured start. Focus on themes that resonate with your current life stage—faith, purity, and courage are just a few examples. Start with one verse a week, gradually building up as you gain confidence.

Here's a simple plan to kick off your challenge:

- **Week 1: Faith**
  Hebrews 11:1, "Now faith is confidence in what we hope for and assurance about what we do not see."

- **Week 2: Purity**
  Psalm 119:9, "How can a young person stay on the path of purity? By living according to your word."

- **Week 3: Courage**
  Joshua 1:9, "Have I not commanded you? Be strong and courageous. Do not be afraid; do not be discouraged, for the Lord your God will be with you wherever you go."

- **Week 4: Strength**
  Isaiah 41:10, "So do not fear, for I am with you; do not be dismayed, for I am your God. I will strengthen, help, and uphold you with my righteous right hand."

By the end of the month, you'll have memorized these four impactful verses and established a habit that will enrich and direct your spiritual journey. Each verse memorized is a step deeper into the heart of God's Word, and each repetition is a stride towards a more resilient and faith-filled life. As you continue this practice, watch how these verses come to life in your daily experiences, transforming your mind, actions, and reactions, aligning them more closely with God's will and ways.

4.3 UNDERSTANDING THE BIBLE: CONTEXT AND CLARITY FOR TEENS

Exploring the Bible can often feel like entering an expansive, ancient universe with its own rules, characters, and landscapes. It's filled with poetry, narratives, laws, prophecies, and letters, each serving a unique purpose in the biblical story. Understanding these different genres is crucial because each one communicates in its way. For instance, poetic books like Psalms express emotion and truth through verse, using metaphor and rhythm to convey profound spiritual truths. Historical books, such as 1 and 2 Kings, provide a narrative account of Israel's history, offering insights into God's relationship with His people through actual events. Prophetic books like Isaiah and Jeremiah use symbolic language and visions to convey messages of warning and hope from God to His people.

However, it's not solely about identifying these genres. Historical narratives are best read with an eye for the overarching story of God's redemption, while poetic books often require contemplation to appreciate their beauty and depth. On the other hand, prophecies require us to understand their original context—who the intended audience was, why they were written, and the immediate implications. It prevents misinterpretations by taking verses out of context and using them unintendedly.

Understanding any part of the Bible requires considering its context. Each book comes from a specific historical and cultural setting that profoundly influences its content and message. For instance, knowing the cultural significance of covenant ceremonies in ancient Near Eastern culture can illuminate Genesis passages describing God's covenants with His people. Understanding the oppressive political conditions when the New Testament was written can illuminate the radical nature of Jesus' teachings about power and servitude.

Many resources are available if you're interested in exploring the Bible more fully. Study Bibles are a great starting point because they provide detailed notes, maps, and commentary alongside the scriptures, making accessing historical and cultural insights easier.

Commentaries offer more in-depth analysis and are invaluable for understanding difficult passages. Online resources provide convenient access to scholarly articles, language tools, and historical data that enhance the understanding of biblical text. Platforms like Bible Gateway and Blue Letter

Bible combine scripture access and study tools, making them convenient for quick searches and in-depth study sessions.

Lastly, the journey of comprehending the Bible is meant to be shared, not solitary. Asking questions and sharing insights with others can enhance your understanding and faith. Engaging in conversations with others, whether in a Bible study group, with a mentor, or online forums, can bring new perspectives and deeper insights.

By understanding the genres, context, and available resources, the Bible becomes a rich source of wisdom and life instead of a daunting collection of ancient texts. As you continue to explore, remember that each page invites you into a deeper relationship with God, offering His truths and promises to guide and enrich your life.

4.4 PRAYER AS CONVERSATION: TALKING TO GOD AS A FRIEND

Imagine sitting at a cozy coffee shop across from someone who knows you thoroughly and loves you unconditionally. That's the essence of prayer—**a heart-to-heart conversation with God**, your heavenly Father. This change in perspective turns prayer into a welcoming and enriching dialogue rather than a formal ritual. It's not about reciting perfect words; it's about sharing your true self with God, who is eager to listen and speak with you.

In the Garden of Gethsemane, Jesus gave us a profound example of conversational prayer just before His crucifixion. He stepped away from His disciples, knelt, and poured out His deepest fears and desires to God, saying, **"Abba, Father, all things are possible for you. Take this cup from me. Yet not what I will, but what you will"** (Mark 14:36).

Using "Abba," which translates to "Daddy," this intimate address shows Jesus's closeness with His Father. It was a raw, honest prayer expressing His human hesitations but ultimately surrendering to God's plan. This model shows us that worship isn't about formalities; it's about opening your heart to God as Jesus did, sharing your fears, hopes, and joys.

So, what can you say in your prayers? Begin by expressing your thoughts. It could be something as simple as your feelings about an upcoming exam, concerns about a friend, or excitement about a new opportunity. God cares about every detail, no matter how trivial it might seem. For instance, if you're worried about a presentation, tell Him about it. Ask for confidence and peace. If you're grateful for a beautiful day or a good laugh with a friend, thank Him for those moments. This ongoing conversation helps build a relationship where you can see God as a sovereign Lord and a loving Father who delights in hearing from you.

Listening is an essential part of any conversation, including your prayer life. But how do you hear God's responses? Often, His voice isn't audible but comes through Scripture, thoughts, emotions, or even the advice of others. After sharing your thoughts with God, spend some time in silence, allowing Him to speak to your heart. You might feel prompted to read a specific passage from the Bible or recall a verse that suddenly seems relevant. Sometimes, it's a sense of peace or an inexplicable confidence that wasn't there before. Recognizing God's responses comes from having a tuned heart, being familiar with His Word, and being sensitive to the Holy Spirit's subtle movements within you.

Reflective Listening Exercise

Try this simple exercise to practice listening during your prayer time. After you've shared your thoughts with God, open your Bible to a book like Psalms or one of the Gospels. Read slowly, pausing frequently to reflect on each verse. Should a specific verse capture your interest, pause and contemplate the reason behind its impact. What is God saying to you through these words? How do they relate to what you've just prayed about? Jot down your thoughts and any actions you feel compelled to take. This practice can help you connect your conversation with God to your daily life, making His Word a direct answer to your prayers.

Embracing prayer as a conversation with God transforms your faith experience from a religious obligation to a dynamic relationship. It turns every prayer time into an opportunity to deepen your understanding of God and how He works. The more you engage in conversation with God daily, the more you'll realize that this heavenly dialogue is a crucial source of **strength, guidance, and comfort,** regardless of your challenges.

4.5 FAITH IN ACTION: LIVING OUT THE BEATITUDES

Picture your daily life as a canvas; every action and choice adds to a bigger picture. Imagine the Beatitudes, the profound blessings Jesus spoke in Matthew 5 during the Sermon on the Mount, influencing each brushstroke.

These aren't just lofty spiritual ideals; they're practical signposts for living a life that reflects your faith in real and tangible ways. The Beatitudes start with **"Blessed are the poor in spirit, for theirs is the kingdom of heaven,"** setting a tone of humility and recognizing our need for God. Each subsequent Beatitude—whether it's those who mourn, the meek, or those who hunger and thirst for righteousness—highlights attributes that align closely with Christ's teachings and character.

They call us to live in ways that might seem countercultural, prioritizing spiritual richness over worldly success, showing strength through gentleness, and finding comfort in God's promises.

Practicing the Beatitudes can lead to beautiful transformation, affecting your inner life and interactions with the world. For example, **"Blessed are the peacemakers, for they will be called children of God."** As a peacemaker, you can mediate disputes among your friends with grace and wisdom, striving to heal divisions rather than make them worse. It could also look like stepping into broader community or school conflicts, not with contentious words but with actions and intentions that promote reconciliation and understanding. The peace advocated for here is more than just a lack of conflict.

The internal rewards of living out the Beatitudes are profound. Embodying these principles brings peace and fulfillment from aligning your actions with your beliefs. It deepens your relationship with God as you live out the traits

Jesus taught and exemplified. You can feel the significance of the external impact equally when you look at it.

These actions build bridges, heal old wounds, and forge strong, meaningful relationships. They can transform not just your perspective but also the hearts of those around you, spreading hope and light in your circles and beyond.

Incorporating the Beatitudes into your life also opens opportunities for engaging in community service projects aligning with these values. Volunteering at a local homeless shelter practically embodies the call to mercy in **"Blessed are the merciful, for they will be shown mercy."** Here, you're not just providing a meal or a bed; you're offering dignity and compassion, recognizing God's face in those often overlooked. Arranging a community clean-up supports the Beatitude's message of being custodians of the earth and demonstrating God's love by caring for His creation. Each act of service, guided by the Beatitudes, not only meets immediate needs but also sows seeds of love, justice, and peace in your community.

By taking these actions, the Beatitudes go beyond mere words in the Bible. They move you to act, speak, and love in ways that echo Jesus' ministry.

Each step you take in embodying these blessings helps paint that larger picture on your life's canvas—one that vividly expresses the beauty, challenge, and joy of walking in faith and living out the truths of the gospel. By consistently applying these timeless principles, you will see how they enhance your life and impact and build a lasting legacy of faith rooted in Christ's teachings.

Whether you are comforting a friend in distress, showing humility in a competitive environment, or extending forgiveness where it's hard, you are living the Beatitudes, and every act is a testament to the transformative power of living a life that truly reflects the heart of the gospel.

4.6 QUESTIONS & ANSWERS: NAVIGATING DOUBTS IN YOUR FAITH JOURNEY

Facing doubts in your faith doesn't mean you're losing belief; instead, it's a sign that you're engaging deeply with your spirituality, wrestling with big questions, and growing in understanding. Doubt is a common experience for many believers, including some of the most faithful figures in the Bible. It's part of developing a mature, robust faith that can stand firm in the realities of life. Consider the challenges and doubts as exercises that strengthen your faith, similar to how muscles grow.

Take, for instance, Thomas, often dubbed **"Doubting Thomas,"** who wouldn't believe in Jesus' resurrection until he could see and touch Christ's wounds. This biblical story isn't just about doubt; it's about how Jesus responded to that doubt—not with rebuke but with compassion, allowing Thomas to explore his doubts by offering proof of His resurrected body. This encounter transformed Thomas's faith, turning his doubt into a declaration of belief as he exclaimed, **"My Lord and my God!"** (John 20:28).

Similarly, even after a tremendous victory at Mount Carmel, the prophet Elijah was overwhelmed by doubt and fear. God's response was to meet Elijah in a gentle whisper, addressing his spiritual needs and reaffirming his mission. These stories teach us that God doesn't turn away from us in our moments of doubt; He draws closer, ready to guide us.

Creating a safe space for questions and doubts is crucial to your faith journey. In your journal, jot down your doubts and questions. Once you've articulated these thoughts, pray to God, asking for His guidance and wisdom. Then, actively seek answers through scripture study, which can shed light on your doubts and offer new insights. Engaging with trusted mentors or friends about these questions can also be helpful. Open discussions can provide different perspectives and encourage your search for answers, reminding you that you're not alone in your doubts.

Consider resources designed to address common doubts and theological challenges for tough questions. Books like **The Case for Christ** by Lee Strobel and **Mere Christianity** by C.S. Lewis offer valuable insights. Podcasts like **The Bible Project** explain biblical themes accessibly, while websites like **GotQuestions.org** provide concise answers to various faith-related questions.

As you navigate your doubts, remember that they don't define your faith—they refine it. Every question you explore and every uncertainty you face leads to greater understanding and a stronger, more personal conviction. Embrace this part of your spiritual journey, knowing that deeper conviction and renewed commitment to your beliefs often lie on the other side of doubt.

ACTIVITY - CHAPTER 4

Scan the QR code

Chapter 5

Overcoming Life's Challenges with Biblical Wisdom

Imagine you're at school, weaving through busy hallways filled with laughter, chatter, and occasional whispers. It's like walking through a marketplace of ideas and emotions, where every corner presents a new challenge or opportunity. This chapter serves as your roadmap for gracefully and wisely navigating the marketplace, utilizing biblical teachings to tackle real-life issues like bullying, which unfortunately impacts many individuals. Here, you'll discover how to handle such trials with resilience and a spirit of kindness and courage that reflects the heart of Jesus.

5.1 HANDLING BULLYING WITH KINDNESS AND COURAGE

In the Sermon on the Mount, Jesus presents a radical call: ***"But I tell you, love your enemies and pray for those who persecute you"*** (Matthew 5:44). This teaching might sound impractical in the face of bullying, where our instinct might be to retaliate or withdraw. Nevertheless, implementing these principles can empower you to confront and overcome bullying with gentleness and resilience.

Consider the story of Joseph, found in the Book of Genesis. Joseph was not only bullied but betrayed by his brothers, thrown into a pit, and sold into slavery. Despite these extreme hardships, Joseph's response was not vengeance but forgiveness and leadership. He rose to power in Egypt, saving his brothers during a famine. Even when faced with severe adversity, Joseph's resilience and forgiveness never wavered. His story teaches us that our response to bullying can transcend the immediate hurt and lead to more significant growth and reconciliation.

How can you apply these biblical lessons to real-life bullying scenarios? First, practicing assertive communication involves expressing your feelings clearly and respectfully. This approach allows you to stand up for yourself without being passive or aggressive. Let's say someone says something hurtful; you can respond calmly, **"That comment was hurtful, and it would be great if you could avoid saying things like that to me."** This approach not only respects your dignity and the dignity of the offending person but also reflects the respect Jesus showed to those who opposed him.

Seeking help from trusted adults is another vital strategy. Reporting bullying can sometimes feel daunting, but remember; God places people in our lives to help us. Proverbs 15:22 says, **"Plans fail for lack of counsel, but with many advisers they succeed."** Whether it's a teacher, counselor, or family member, sharing your experiences can give you the support and guidance needed to navigate the situation effectively, making you feel supported and guided.

Additionally, fostering a supportive peer environment is essential. This involves standing up for those bullied and encouraging a culture that values kindness and acceptance. As a Christian, you have a unique role in fostering this environment. By showing love and support to others, you can help deter bullying behavior and build a community that reflects the values of Christ's teachings. It might involve starting or participating in anti-bullying programs at school or simply being a friend to someone in need, making you feel responsible and influential.

Engaging Exercise: Role-Playing Scenarios

Participate in role-playing activities with friends or family to strengthen your skills in dealing with bullying. Create scenarios based on everyday bullying situations and practice responding with assertiveness and compassion. This exercise helps you handle real-life situations and boosts your confidence in communication and standing up for yourself and others, all while honoring God.

Handling bullying with kindness and courage is not about condoning the behavior or being a passive victim. It's about **rising above** the situation, armed with the wisdom and love that come from your faith. By addressing bullying in line with biblical principles, you not only preserve your dignity but also create an opportunity for healing and potentially changing the behavior of the person causing harm. Remember, each challenge you face is an opportunity to demonstrate the transformative power of God's love, turning situations meant for harm into stories of grace and strength.

5.2 DEALING WITH ACADEMIC PRESSURE: LEARNING FROM DANIEL

Just imagine yourself in ancient Babylon, embraced by the grandeur of a royal court, challenged to excel in foreign studies and responsibilities, just like Daniel from the Bible. Thrust into a high-pressure environment after being taken from his home, Daniel faced immense academic and social challenges. Yet he survived; he thrived, showing extraordinary commitment and wisdom. *"To these four young men, God gave knowledge and understanding of all kinds of literature and learning. And Daniel could understand visions and dreams of all kinds. In every matter of wisdom and understanding about which the king questioned them, he found them ten times better than all the magicians and enchanters in his whole kingdom"* (Daniel 1:17-20).

Daniel's story is a testament to balancing responsibilities while deeply rooted in faith. It highlights that turning to **God's wisdom** in times of tremendous pressure can bring exceptional triumph, even in unfamiliar or challenging circumstances.

Daniel's secret to excelling under pressure was his unwavering faith in God, from whom he sought wisdom continually. This reliance on divine insight is crucial for you, too, especially when academic challenges seem insurmountable. When subjects are complex, or the fear of exams looms significant, remember that wisdom doesn't just come from textbooks; it comes from God, *"who gives generously to all without finding fault"* (James 1:5).

Make it a habit to start your study sessions with a prayer for understanding, asking God to open your mind and guide your learning. This practice sets a tone of reliance on God's strength, not just your efforts, and can transform your study time into an act of worship.

Effective time management is another critical area where biblical principles can guide you. Ecclesiastes 3:1 tells us, **"There is a time for everything and a season for every activity under the heavens."** This wisdom from Solomon highlights the importance of creating balance in your life.

Start by prioritizing your tasks, from the most urgent and essential to those that can wait. Use a planner or digital app to keep track of assignments, tests, and other commitments. Break larger tasks into smaller, manageable chunks to stay organized and prevent feeling overwhelmed. This approach helps you see what you need to do and when. Also, remember to set aside time for rest and spiritual growth. Just as **"Jesus often withdrew to lonely places and prayed"** (Luke 5:16), you also need regular breaks to rejuvenate spiritually and mentally.

Maintaining a healthy perspective on success is equally important. In a culture that often equates achievement with self-worth, it's vital to remember that grades or accolades do not define your value. Despite Daniel's conventional success, his story highlights that his true worth came from his relationship with God, not his academic accomplishments. You are valued beyond your performance on any test or assignment. Celebrate your efforts regardless of the outcome, knowing that each step of your educational journey is an opportunity to learn and grow, not just a means to an end. **Embrace a balanced view of success, including personal development, relationships, spiritual growth, and academic achievements.**

Reflective Exercise: Time Management Audit

For practical application, think about doing a weekly time management audit. Over the next week, keep a detailed log of how you spend your time, from schoolwork to social activities, including how much time you spend in prayer and other spiritual practices. Review your log at the end of the week and ask yourself: Are there areas where I can cut back or redistribute time to reduce stress? Am I allocating time for God and my spiritual growth?

Through this exercise, you can discover essential revelations about how your time is aligned with your priorities and make improvements for a more balanced and fulfilling life.

Navigating academic pressures with faith and wisdom is not about striving for perfection but **peace and purpose** in your educational journey. Like Daniel, you can excel in your studies while keeping your faith at the forefront, using each challenge as an opportunity to deepen your reliance on God's wisdom. **Each day presents a fresh chance to embrace faith, balance, and perseverance,** transforming academic pressure into a path toward growth and accomplishment. As you continue to navigate your educational path, carry with you the lessons from Daniel's life, knowing that you have access to an unending source of wisdom and strength with God.

5.3 BODY IMAGE: WHAT WOULD ESTHER THINK?

When we delve into the story of Esther, we find a young woman whose beauty was undeniable, a critical factor in her rise to queenhood. Yet, it would be a mistake to see her physical appearance as the sole reason for her success or her primary attribute. Esther's true beauty lay in her **courageousness and sharp decision-making**, which allowed her to rescue her people from destruction. Her story in the Bible unfolds as one of courage and strategic intelligence, showing us that while her beauty opened doors, **her faith and wisdom** were what truly made a difference. This dual portrayal helps us understand that our physical attributes are just parts of a larger picture of who we are and what we can achieve.

In today's society, there's a relentless barrage of messages suggesting that physical beauty equates to worth and success. The constant messages from billboards, TV screens, and social media can distort how we see ourselves and our values. However, the biblical view presented in 1 Peter 3:3-4 urges us to focus on the **"unfading beauty of a gentle and quiet spirit, which is of great worth in God's sight."** This scripture doesn't diminish the value of outer beauty but emphasizes that inner beauty—the quality of our hearts and the strength of our spirits—is far more precious and enduring. This perspective promotes the development of qualities such as **kindness, empathy, and courage,** which embody everlasting beauty.

Promoting a healthy self-image involves more than rejecting unrealistic beauty standards; it's about embracing a lifestyle that celebrates all aspects of our being. One way to foster this is by focusing on self-care practices that **nourish the body, soul, and mind.** Activities like exercise, healthy eating, and adequate rest are essential, but **prayer, meditation, and engaging in activities that bring joy and satisfaction** are equally crucial. Another essential practice is cultivating gratitude—specifically, gratitude for what your body can do rather than how it looks.

For example, you might thank your legs for carrying you through a busy day, your arms for allowing you to hug loved ones, or your senses for letting you experience the world in vivid detail. By shifting our focus from appearance to abilities, we can see our bodies as divine instruments rather than objects.

Additionally, we should pay attention to the influence of role models on our perception of beauty and self-esteem. In the Christian community, many women use their platforms to advocate for a healthy body image and inspire confidence in our identity in Christ. These women, from authors and speakers to leaders and everyday believers, share their journeys of embracing their

God-given design and finding their worth in their faith rather than their physical appearance. Their stories are not just inspiring; they offer practical insights and affirmations that can empower us to view ourselves through a lens of divine love and acceptance. By recognizing these inspiring individuals and aiming to emulate them, we can challenge the harmful narratives prevalent in our culture and promote positive values.

When you feel overwhelmed by the chaotic messages about beauty and worth, think of Esther. Let her story remind you that while the world may focus on the external, **God looks at the heart**, and it is this inner beauty that we are called to cultivate. By embracing practices that feed your body and soul and looking up to spiritual role models, you can form a healthy self-image and authentically rooted in your identity in Christ. Let this understanding shape how you see yourself and others, fostering an environment where true beauty—**the beauty of a life lived in faith and love—is recognized and celebrated.**

5.4 NAVIGATING SOCIAL MEDIA: LESSONS FROM PAUL'S LETTERS

With the rapid exchange of tweets and carefully curated Instagram feeds (or any other active forums), anchoring our online interactions in enduring truths is increasingly essential. Though penned in a time far removed from our digital world, Paul's letters offer timeless wisdom on communicating in ways that honor God and reflect His love. In Ephesians 4:15, Paul urges us to **"speak the truth in love,"** a principle that can transform our digital dialogues. This guidance prompts us to consider what we post and how. Is your comment truthful? Is it expressed with love and consideration for the person on the other side of the screen?

Applying this principle might mean taking a moment to pause before responding to a post that upsets you. In that pause, ask yourself if your response is accurate and kind. It doesn't mean shying away from honest conversations or avoiding complex topics; instead, it's about ensuring that **your contributions promote understanding and respect** rather than conflict. This approach can prevent misunderstandings and build bridges in conversations, making your social media spaces more welcoming and cheerful.

Discernment is critical to navigating social media effectively. Philippians 4:8 offers a perfect filter for online engagement: whatever is true, noble, correct, pure, lovely, and admirable—these are the things to think about and share. Use this verse as your checklist when deciding whether to share a particular content. Does this post uplift and inspire? Does it encourage critical thinking and positive action? Is it respectful to all people involved? Filtering your content through these questions can help you maintain a testimony online that aligns with your values.

Moreover, the digital footprint you create through your posts, comments, and shares forms a lasting image of who you are. It's important to remember that what you share online can remain in the digital sphere forever. This permanence should be a reminder to handle your online presence responsibly. Consider how your posts today might be perceived years from now. Are they posts you'd be proud of? Do they represent the kind of person you aspire to be? It's about avoiding negative consequences and ensuring your digital presence reflects your Christian values.

Encouraging positive online evangelism is another significant way to use social media to reflect Christ's love. Platforms like Instagram or Facebook can be more than just spaces for sharing personal updates; they can be powerful tools for spreading the gospel and positive messages. **Highlight stories of faith, share verses that inspire you, or post about community service projects.** These posts can serve as beacons of hope and encouragement to others. Additionally, supporting and sharing content from Christian influencers who promote biblical truths and godly living can amplify the impact of positive messaging. These influencers often tackle real-life issues from a faith-based perspective, guiding and encouraging their followers. By engaging with and sharing their content, you help extend their reach, spreading messages that uplift and inspire a wider audience.

Embracing Paul's wisdom enables us to elevate our online interactions from ordinary to profound. It encourages us to create a digital presence that reflects our faith and fosters a community that uplifts and edifies. As you post, comment, and share, remember that each interaction is an opportunity to demonstrate the grace and truth of God's love. Let your digital footprint lead others toward kindness, understanding, and faith.

5.5 Overcoming Fear of the Future: The Story of Joseph

Reflecting on Joseph's life, it's clear that his journey was anything but straightforward. Joseph's path was marked by uncertainty and fear as he went from beloved son to betrayed brother, slave to prisoner, and ultimately, governor of Egypt. Yet, his faith in God's plan never wavered through it all. Joseph believed God guided him towards a greater purpose despite an uncertain future. He didn't base his trust on the clarity of his circumstances but on his unwavering belief in **God's sovereignty.**

In Romans 8:28, we find a promise that **"in all things God works for the good of those who love him, who have been called according to his purpose."** This verse doesn't mean that everything that happens to us is good, but it assures us that God can use every situation for our ultimate good. It is similar to Joseph's life, where every misfortune and setback was a stepping stone to fulfilling a greater plan for him and an entire nation. This promise can be your anchor when uncertainty about your future arises. It reassures you that God is not only aware of your situation but is actively working within it, turning your fears and failures into opportunities for growth and blessing.

Let's consider the power of prayer in dealing with fears about the future. Prayer allows you to surrender your anxieties to God, acknowledging His control over your life and future. Here's a guided prayer to help you release your worries and deepen your trust in God's timing and plans:

"Dear Lord, I come to You with a heart full of dreams and a mind full of worries. Sometimes, fearing what lies ahead makes it hard to enjoy the present or learn from the past. I know You hold my future, and I pray for the

courage to trust You. Help me see my life through Your eyes and recognize every challenge as an opportunity to grow closer to You. Teach me to rest in Your promises, knowing that You work all things for my good. Thank you for being my guide and my peace. In Jesus' Name, Amen."

This prayer isn't just words; it's a declaration of your trust in God. It's a commitment to view your future not as a source of fear but as a horizon of hope, knowing that God is already there, preparing the way for you. As you continue to navigate the uncertainties of life, let Joseph's story remind you that no matter how unpredictable your path may seem, your faith can remain constant. Trust in God's sovereignty and presence in every moment, and you'll find that fear has no foothold in the face of such profound assurance. Be receptive to the daily lessons and let your journal and prayers testify to God's constant faithfulness in every step of your journey.

5.6 MAINTAINING PURITY IN A HYPER-SEXUALIZED WORLD

In a society that often bombards us with images and messages that can warp our understanding of sexuality, maintaining Purity can feel like swimming against a powerful current. The challenge isn't just in resisting external pressures; it's about nurturing a view of Purity that reflects your relationship with God and honors Him with your body and actions. In 1 Corinthians 6:18-20, we find a powerful reminder of why our bodies and how we use them matter to God: **"Flee from sexual immorality. All other sins a person commits are outside the body, but whoever sins sexually sins against their own body. Do you not know that your bodies are temples of the Holy Spirit, who is in you, whom you have received from God? You are not your own; you were bought at a price. Therefore, honor God with your bodies."** This scripture doesn't just call us to avoid specific actions; it invites us to view our bodies as sacred, entrusted to us by God, and to live in a way that reflects His love and holiness.

Setting clear boundaries is a crucial step in maintaining this **Purity**. It's about being aware of your standpoint on some issues and being able to lovingly and confidently convey it to others. To establish these boundaries, reflect on your beliefs and their biblical basis through self-reflection and prayer. Once you set these boundaries in your heart, it's essential to communicate them.

It could be as simple as deciding not to be alone in a house with your boyfriend or limiting how late you text or chat online with someone interested. These guidelines are not without purpose; they protect you from situations that may test your dedication to Purity.

In this context, **accountability** plays a vital role. It can be challenging to uphold your standards yourself, but having reliable friends or mentors with similar values can make a big difference.

These accountability partners can offer encouragement, share their experiences, and remind you of your commitment when struggling. They're not there to judge or police you but to support you in living out your faith authentically. Maintaining regular conversations with trusted individuals can offer the reinforcement and perspective necessary to stay true to your path of Purity, particularly when confronted with challenges or temptations.

Promote Accountability and Support

Being part of a youth group or a Christian community that upholds these values can also provide a broader support network. These groups often discuss Purity-related challenges and offer biblical guidance on navigating them. They can also be a source of friendship and fun in a way that honors God, providing alternatives to risky behaviors that might seem like the only social options. Activities like group outings, service projects, and Bible study sessions keep you engaged and surround you with peers walking a similar path, reinforcing that you're not alone in your choices.

Maintaining Purity in a hyper-sexualized world is not about isolating yourself from society or living in fear of making mistakes. It's about making **daily conscious choices that align with your faith and reflect your love for God**. It's about setting boundaries that protect and preserve the incredible value God places on you and your body. It's about building a community that embraces Purity as a joyful expression of God's intention for our lives and supporting each other in this commitment. As you continue to navigate these challenges, remember that you are empowered by the Holy Spirit and supported by a community that values and strives for Purity just as you do.

ACTIVITY - CHAPTER 5

Scan the QR code.

Chapter 6

Encouraging Personal Growth and Self-Discovery

I magine this: You're at a lively fair, buzzing with colors, sounds, and countless booths, each offering something unique and exciting. Picture yourself walking through this fair and being drawn to a booth filled with beautiful, handcrafted instruments. Each one, from the glossy violin to the bold trumpet, produces its distinct sound. Now, think of your life as this fair and your talents and gifts as these instruments. This chapter is about discovering your unique instruments, understanding their rhythms, and learning how to use them to create a beautiful symphony that brings joy and serves a greater purpose.

6.1 Discovering Your Passions: Using Your Gifts for God's Glory

Our talents are gifts from God, placed within us for a purpose beyond just ourselves. These aren't just random skills but unique parts of who we are and what we're passionate about. Discovering these gifts is a joyful journey that starts with looking inward and being honest with ourselves. Think about what activities make you lose track of time or what tasks others often ask you for help with because you're naturally good at them. Whether it's the art of persuasion, the joy of making music, or the knack for solving puzzles, each talent is like a puzzle piece that makes up who you are.

Start your journey of discovery by reflecting on moments when you felt genuinely alive or accomplished something effortlessly. These moments are clues to **your gifts**. Writing them down can be very revealing. Remember, discovering your talents is a process that requires patience. You might also ask your friends and family for feedback—sometimes, they notice our gifts before we do! Trying new activities outside your comfort zone, like joining a drama club, volunteering, or participating in a workshop, can uncover hidden talents.

For Instance, consider Sofia, a 15-year-old who discovered her passion for photography when she borrowed her mom's camera for a school project. What started as a simple assignment turned into a love for capturing moments. She now uses her photography skills to create inspiring social media posts that spread positivity and encouragement to her peers, glorifying God through her art.

Once you identify your gifts, consider how to use them to glorify God and serve those around you. Doing this lets you fully express your unique talents and make a meaningful impact. For example, **"Each of you should use whatever gift you have received to serve others, as faithful stewards of God's grace in its various forms"** (1 Peter 4:10-11). Whether leading worship with your musical skills, organizing events with your administrative talents, or writing encouraging notes if you have a way with words—there are countless ways to use your gifts for a greater purpose.

Visual Activity: Reflective Journaling Prompt

Journaling Activity: Create a dedicated page in your journal titled **"Gifts I Can Share."** List your talents and brainstorm ways you can use these gifts at home, at school, or in your community. This visual mapping not only highlights your strengths but also inspires action.

Taking inspiration from stories in the Bible can also help you see how varied these gifts can be and their impact. Think about David, a young shepherd whose music soothed King Saul's troubled spirit. His harp-playing wasn't just a hobby; it was a healing ministry. Or consider Bezalel, who God appointed to craft the Tabernacle. His skills weren't just about creating art—they were instrumental in creating a sacred space for worship. These examples show that no gift is too small or ordinary when used for God's glory.

Stay open to where your talents might take you. Sometimes, our gifts lead us to unexpected places or evolve in ways we didn't expect. Embrace these changes, knowing they're part of your unique growth journey. By exploring and using your talents, you enrich your life and bring joy and inspiration to those around you.

6.2 DECISION MAKING: SEEKING GOD'S GUIDANCE IN BIG AND SMALL CHOICES

Making decisions, whether they're about what to study in college or what to do over the weekend, can feel both exciting and overwhelming. It's like standing at a crossroads with many paths ahead, each leading to different adventures. In these moments, seeking God's guidance isn't just helpful—it's crucial. It transforms decision-making from a stressful task into an opportunity to deepen trust and walk with God. When you choose based on biblical principles, you align yourself with God's will and open your heart to His guidance.

According to the Bible, one of the first steps in making decisions is seeking wise counsel. Proverbs 12:15 says, **"The way of fools seems right to them, but the**

wise listen to advice." It doesn't mean you should make decisions solely based on what others think, but rather that you should seek guidance from trusted mentors, friends, and family who share your values. Their insights can help you see things differently and guide you toward decisions that honor God. This support system is crucial in your decision-making journey.

Modern Example: Emma, a 17-year-old, was unsure about whether to join her school's debate team or focus on her part-time job. She sought advice from her youth pastor and her parents, prayed about it, and felt a sense of peace when she decided to join the team. This peace, as described in Colossians 3:15, **"Let the peace of Christ rule in your hearts,"** guided her in making a decision aligned with her values and passions.

Prayer is another essential part of decision-making. It's your direct line to God's wisdom and a way to ask for His guidance. When you pray about your decisions, you're not just seeking answers; you're growing closer to God and becoming more attuned to His voice. Sometimes, God's response might come through a feeling of peace, an unexpected opportunity, or advice from a friend. This peace, as described in Colossians 3:15, is not just a lack of conflict, but a **deep sense of assurance that you are in alignment with God's will**, even if the decision is difficult or the outcome is uncertain.

Reflective Case Study: Esther's Decision

Reflect on Esther's story, particularly in chapters 4 and 5 of the Book of Esther. Faced with the potential destruction of her people, she sought counsel from Mordecai and turned to God through fasting and prayer. Consider her initial hesitation: **"All the king's officials and the people of the royal provinces know that for any man or woman who approaches the king in the inner court without being summoned the king has but one law: that they be put to death unless the king extends the gold scepter to them and spares their lives"** (Esther 4:11). Reflect on the advice she received from Mordecai: **"And who knows but that you have come to your royal position for such a time as this?"** (Esther 4:14), and her faithful decision to act: **"Go, gather together all** the Jews... and fast for me... When this is done, I will go to the king, even though it is against the law. And if I perish, I perish" (Esther 4:16).

How can you apply Esther's approach to decision-making in your own life? Write down your thoughts and any steps you plan to take to align your decisions with these biblical principles.

Visual Activity: Decision-Making Flowchart Inspired by Esther's Story

Create a decision-making flowchart in your journal based on Esther's journey. Follow these steps:

1. Draw a series of boxes connected by arrows.

2. Label each box with the steps from Esther's story:

   ○ (Esther 4:10-11) **"Initial Hesitation"**

   ○ (Esther 4:12-14) **"Seeking Counsel from Mordecai"**

   ○ (Esther 4:15-17) **"Fasting and Praying"**

   ○ **"Taking Action with Courage"**

3. Create your own parallel steps based on a current decision you're facing.

4. Use this flowchart to guide your thought process, identify wise counsel, and encourage prayerful reflection before making a choice.

Remember: Each decision you face, big or small, is an opportunity to grow in faith and wisdom. By keeping biblical examples in mind, you can make choices that lead to good outcomes and strengthen your relationship with God.

6.3 TIME MANAGEMENT: BALANCING LIFE WITH BIBLICAL PRINCIPLES

Do you ever feel like there needs to be more time in the day to do everything you want? It's like being in a boat, paddling against the current, trying to reach the shore before the sun sets. This feeling often isn't just about having too much to do; it's about knowing how to manage the time you have. Ephesians 5:15-16 encourages us to **"Be very careful, then, how you live—not as unwise but as wise, making the most of every opportunity."** This reminder is that time is a precious gift from God, meant to be used wisely.

Start managing your time by prioritizing your tasks. Imagine your daily activities as a set of bins you need to fill. Some bins, like schoolwork or family time, need to be filled daily and take up a lot of space. Others, like hobbies or hanging out with friends, are smaller. By filling the big bins first—your most important tasks—you ensure your priorities are in order. This way, you're not left scrambling to complete crucial tasks at the last minute.

Procrastination can make time management more effortless. Putting off tasks that seem tedious or challenging is tempting, but doing so often leads to stress. To avoid procrastination, break big tasks into smaller, manageable steps. Instead of writing "finish history project" on your to-do list, break it down into steps like "research topic," "create an outline," and "write the first draft." It makes tasks feel less overwhelming and helps you get started.

Modern Example: Mia, a 16-year-old, was constantly overwhelmed with schoolwork and extracurriculars. After reading about time blocking in a productivity book, she decided to try it. By setting specific times for each task and including breaks, she balanced her schedule better and found more time for her hobbies and Bible study.

Practical Tip: Time Blocking

Use time blocking to divide your day into chunks for specific tasks. For example, set aside 30 minutes for a "research topic" and set a timer. This approach makes tasks feel more manageable and adds a bit of fun by turning them into a race against the clock. Knowing you have a set time helps you stay focused and productive.

6.4 FACING FAILURE: LESSONS ON RESILIENCE FROM PETER

Close your eyes and imagine being in a play, standing under the bright stage lights, ready to recite your lines. But then, the words slip away from your memory at the crucial moment. The silence feels overwhelming. It's a moment of failure, and it stings. Yet, it's also a moment filled with potential—for growth, learning, and resilience. Just like in a play, life doesn't always go perfectly. Despite our best efforts, we all face moments when things don't go as planned. Failure doesn't diminish your worth or mean God is disappointed in you. Instead, it's a shared human experience, a chapter in everyone's story, **and it's not the end of yours.**

Consider Peter, one of Jesus' closest disciples. Peter was known for his passion and courage, but he also experienced significant failures. His most notable mistake was denying Jesus—not just once, but three times—despite confidently declaring he would never abandon Him. This moment of weakness could have defined Peter's life as a betrayal. However, what happened next is a powerful reminder of **God's grace and forgiveness.**

After His resurrection, Jesus accepted Peter; instead, He gently restored him. Jesus asked Peter three times if he loved Him, mirroring Peter's three denials. Each affirmation of love was a step toward healing Peter's heart and recommissioning him for future service. This story shows us that we can overcome mistakes, which leads to restoration and growth. Our failures often serve as a fertile ground where we plant seeds of **deeper faith and understanding.**

Modern Example: Think of Lana, a high school junior who missed a crucial shot in the basketball finals. She felt like she had let her entire team down. However, instead of giving up, Lana used that experience to train harder, improve her skills, and build resilience. She also learned to lean on her faith, trusting that her worth wasn't defined by one missed shot but by who she was in God's eyes.

In moments of failure, resilience becomes your greatest ally. Scripture is rich with verses that reinforce the promise of God's support and strength during such times. Psalm 34:18 reminds us, **"The Lord is close to the brokenhearted and saves those who are crushed in spirit."** This verse doesn't just offer comfort; it assures you of God's presence right in the middle of your struggles.

Another encouraging scripture is James 4:6, **"But he gives more grace. Therefore, it says, 'God opposes the proud, but gives grace to the humble."** Here, we learn that humility, which often grows from failure, draws God's grace. It's a divine formula that turns our setbacks into opportunities for His grace to shine.

Adopting a growth mindset is critical to transforming how you view and respond to failures. This mindset shifts your focus from what you've lost to what you can learn from each experience. **Every failure teaches a lesson;** it's a stepping stone, not a stumbling block. Instead of asking, "Why did this happen to me?" try asking, **"What can I learn from this?"**

Visual Activity: Growth Mindset Reflection Chart

Create a "Growth Mindset Reflection Chart" in your journal. Follow these steps:

1. Divide the page into three columns:

    o **"What Happened?"**

    o **"How Did I Feel?"**

    o **"What Did I Learn?"**

2. **Use this chart** to reflect on a recent experience where things didn't go as planned.

Perseverance plays a crucial role in this process. It's the determination to keep moving forward, try again, learn, and grow despite setbacks. Romans 5:3-4 beautifully captures this process: **"Not only so, but we also glory in**

our sufferings, because we know that suffering produces perseverance; perseverance, character; and character, hope." These words describe a journey of transformation where each challenge and failure builds a character that is hopeful, resilient, and anchored in God's promises.

Failures, big or small, don't define your journey. They do not determine your worth but show your progress. Embrace these moments with grace and resilience, for they shape you into someone with a more robust character, deeper faith, and significant impact. Let your failures be your teacher, not your tormentor, guiding you to a fuller understanding of yourself and the abundant grace that God provides.

6.5 THE ART OF PATIENCE: WAITING ON GOD'S TIMING

Have you ever felt stuck in a situation where time seems to stand still and nothing seems to change? It's like watching a pot, waiting for it to boil, but it feels like it's taking forever. We've all been there, and it's in these moments that we struggle with impatience. But what if these waiting periods are not empty gaps in our lives? What if they are rich opportunities for growth and deepening our faith? Waiting is a vital part of God's plan—a divine pause that prepares us for what's to come. This waiting isn't passive; we cultivate patience and strengthen our trust in God's timing.

Consider the story of Abraham, a central figure in the Bible, who God promised that he would be the father of many nations. However, this promise took time to happen. Abraham waited for years, even decades until his wife Sarah finally gave birth to their son Isaac. During this waiting period, Abraham sometimes doubted and even made mistakes, but we celebrate his journey as a testament to faith and patience. His experience teaches us that human timelines do not bind God's promises. They often require a journey of waiting, which strengthens our belief and teaches us patience.

Modern Example: Think about Lisa, a senior in high school waiting to hear back from her top college choices. Although she felt anxious and impatient during this waiting period, she volunteered at a local shelter and deepened her prayer life. Ultimately, she found peace in trusting God's plan, no matter the outcome. This waiting period became a time of personal growth and spiritual strengthening.

Similarly, again the story of Joseph illustrates how a dream can take a winding road before coming true. Joseph's journey—from being sold into slavery by his brothers to rising to power in Egypt—was filled with injustice and hardship. Yet, Joseph remained patient and steadfast in his faith. His ability to wait on God's timing was crucial. Joseph's moment came when he saved Egypt from famine and reconciled with his family, repairing broken relationships. His patience and trust in God's plan were critical to his story and the larger narrative of the Israelites.

Interactive Activity: Patience Journal

Start a **"Patience Journal."** Each day, write about a situation where you felt impatient. Reflect on what you learned from waiting and how you can apply that lesson to future conditions. Also, jot down any scriptures or prayers that help you during these waiting times.

Visual Activity: Journal Page Layout for Documenting Experiences and Insights

Design a journal page layout to document your experiences and insights during periods of waiting. Divide the page into three sections:

1. **"What Am I Waiting For?"**

   o Describe what you are currently waiting for.

2. **"Feelings and Challenges"**

   o Write down your emotions and any struggles you're facing during this waiting period.

3. **"Lessons Learned and Growth Opportunities"**

   o Reflect on the lessons you're learning and how you are growing through the experience.

Developing patience, especially in today's fast-paced world, can seem challenging, but it is possible. One practical way to cultivate patience is by meditating on Scripture. It involves more than just reading the Bible; it's about letting the words seep into your heart and mind, reflecting on them, and letting them shape your perspective. For example, meditating on Romans 12:12, **"Be joyful in hope, patient in affliction, faithful in prayer,"** can provide comfort and guidance during waiting times.

Engaging in slow-paced hobbies can also help build patience. Activities like gardening, where you plant a seed and wait for it to grow, or knitting, where each stitch contributes to a larger pattern, can serve as metaphors for spiritual growth. These activities remind us that worthwhile outcomes require time and perseverance, mirroring the spiritual fruits of waiting periods.

Lastly, practicing mindfulness can help increase patience. It means being fully present in the moment, aware of your surroundings, emotions, and thoughts, without rushing to the next item on your to-do list. It's about finding value in the present, even in moments of waiting. **Mindfulness helps you recognize that every season, even those of delay, has purpose and value.**

Encouraging trust in God's plan is essential as you cultivate patience. It's about believing He knows your future and that His timing is perfect, even when it doesn't align with your expectations. When you grow impatient, remember God's faithfulness in past situations. Reflect on times when His timing, though it seemed slow, was perfect. These memories can strengthen your trust during current or future waiting periods.

As you navigate seasons of waiting, remember that patience is not just about passing time. It's about recognizing each moment as part of God's grand design for your life. It's about trusting in His timing, knowing He is weaving every experience into a beautiful tapestry of grace and purpose. Whether you are waiting for an answer, a change, or a dream to come true, let patience tune your heart to God's rhythm. Embrace this season with a heart of expectancy, knowing that what God orchestrates in **His perfect timing will be worth every moment you wait.**

6.6 CULTIVATING GRATITUDE: A DAILY PRACTICE

Gratitude isn't just about saying "thank you" for the big, life-changing moments. It's about noticing the small things—the everyday blessings often overlooked. It could be the warm smile from a friend in the hallway, how your favorite song lifts your mood, or the peaceful quiet during a walk outside. These moments fill your life with meaning, even when things feel overwhelming.

When you make the conscious decision to embrace gratitude, a profound transformation begins. Instead of fixating on what you lack, you start to appreciate the beauty in what you have. This shift in mindset not only elevates your happiness but also diminishes stress, enhances your mental well-being, and fortifies your relationships. Just imagine the depth of connection that can be fostered when someone acknowledges your efforts. Gratitude has the power to enrich these bonds.

Gratitude transcends the material realm. It is a force that strengthens your bond with the divine. When you acknowledge the blessings in your life, you are opening your heart to His presence and discerning His hand in every moment, big or small. As 1 Thessalonians 5:18 reminds us, 'Give thanks in all circumstances; for this is God's will for you in Christ Jesus.' Even on the most challenging days, gratitude serves as a beacon of trust, reminding you that God is guiding you and that every moment, whether joyful or arduous, is part of a grander design.

So, the next time you find yourself in the grip of frustration or stress, take a moment to pause and reflect on the goodness that surrounds you. It could be as simple as a kind word from a friend or a fleeting moment of peace. Maintaining a gratitude journal is an excellent way to document these small blessings. Over time, you'll witness how they accumulate to form a life brimming with meaning and joy. **Gratitude can be your superpower, anchoring you, fostering connections, and infusing joy into every season of life.**

ACTIVITY - CHAPTER 6

Scan the QR code.

Chapter 7

Building a Legacy of Faith and Leadership

Imagine navigating through your high school years as your ship's captain, steering through calm and stormy waters with a clear sense of purpose and unwavering conviction. Just like a captain, your role isn't just to keep the boat afloat, but to guide it with a determined focus. Similarly, being a leader in your own life isn't about holding a position of power; it's about living out your values and inspiring others through your actions. This chapter focuses on what it means to lead with love and faith in everyday moments, reflecting a leadership style rooted deeply in Christian values. Let's explore how to embrace these principles to impact your world meaningfully.

7.1 LEADING WITH LOVE: WHAT IT MEANS TO BE A CHRISTIAN LEADER

Redefining Leadership for Teens

In today's world, leadership is often equated with authority and decision-making. However, Christian leadership presents a unique perspective—**one of service, humility, and selflessness.** True leadership isn't about the number of followers you have; it's about the number of people you serve and how you reflect Christ's love in everything you do.

Learning from Jesus' Example

Consider the moment Jesus washed His disciples' feet (John 13:1-17). Here was the Son of God, performing a task reserved for the lowest servants. In this humble act, Jesus showed us that being a leader is about caring for others in practical, tangible ways. As a teen, you have unique opportunities to lead by Example in your everyday life—whether you help a friend with homework, stand up for someone being teased, or listen to someone who needs it.

Modern Example: Consider Jessica, a 16-year-old who noticed a new student struggling to make friends at school. Instead of ignoring her, Jessica took the initiative to invite her to sit with her group at lunch and introduced her to others. This small act of kindness made a big difference, helping the new student feel welcomed and included. Jessica's actions demonstrated leadership by showing love and care simply yet impactfully.

Small Acts, Big Impact

Leadership is not just about grand gestures; you demonstrate it through your small, everyday decisions. Choosing to be kind, standing up for your beliefs, or offering support to a friend in need are all acts of leadership. These seemingly small actions, when done with love and faith, can have a profound impact on those around you. Think about ways you can lead in your daily life. Could you start a study group for classmates struggling with a subject? Organize a community service project with your youth group. Or be someone others can count on when they need a friend? These actions, though small, can have a profound impact on those around you, empowering you to make a difference in your community.

7.2 PRACTICAL STEPS TO LEAD WITH FAITH

Create a Personal Leadership Action Plan

To help you put these ideas into action, consider creating a "Personal Leadership Plan." Start by identifying one or two small acts of leadership you can practice this week, such as helping a new student feel welcome or volunteering to organize a youth group activity. Write down your goals and reflect on how these actions can help you grow as a leader. Over time, set bigger goals, like starting a peer mentoring program or organizing a charity drive. Keep track of your progress and see how these small steps can lead to meaningful changes in your community and your personal growth.

Modern Example: Take Kaylee, who decided to start a book club at her school focused on reading and discussing books about social justice. She wanted to create a space where students could learn, share, and grow together. Her initiative built a sense of community and encouraged others to think critically and compassionately about the world around them. Through this, Kaylee, led by Example, shows how to combine passion with action.

Encourage Peer Support and Collaboration

You don't have to lead alone. Inviting friends or peers to join you in your leadership journey can be a rewarding experience. Whether it's organizing a community service project or starting a prayer group, collaborating with others not only shares the workload but also creates a sense of community and shared purpose. Working together allows you to support each other, share ideas, and grow together in faith.

Modern Example: Emily, a high school junior, started a peer support group for students struggling with anxiety and stress. She collaborated with friends and a teacher to create a safe space for sharing and support. The group quickly became a source of encouragement and strength, helping students feel less alone and more empowered to face their challenges.

7.3 LIVING OUT YOUR FAITH IN EVERYDAY DECISIONS

Making Faith-Based Choices

You'll face decisions that challenge your values as you navigate school and life. Maybe you're tempted to follow the crowd in a way that conflicts with your beliefs, or perhaps you're facing pressure to compromise your integrity. In these moments, remember that your faith is a guiding light. Leadership is about standing firm in your faith, even when it's difficult. **"No temptation has overtaken you except what is common to mankind. And God is faithful; he will not let you be tempted beyond what you can bear. But when you are tempted, he will also provide a way out so that you can endure it"** (1

Corinthians 10:13). Let your faith be your compass in making decisions, and you will always find the right path.

Reflective Practice: Decision-Making Journal

Consider starting a decision-making journal. When faced with a tough choice, write down your thoughts, the options you have, and how each choice aligns with your values. Reflect on scriptures that offer guidance and pray for wisdom. This practice helps you make decisions with a clear mind and deepens your relationship with God as you seek His guidance in all areas of your life.

Modern Example: Anna, a senior, was offered an opportunity to cheat on a major exam. Instead of giving in, she reflected on her values and prayed for guidance. She decided to study harder and trust in God's provision. Her integrity earned her respect from her peers and strengthened her faith, showing that choosing the right path brings unexpected rewards.

7.4 LEARNING FROM BIBLICAL ROLE MODELS

Drawing Inspiration from Women of the Bible

The Bible is full of stories about incredible women who showed strength, courage, and wisdom through their faith. One of these amazing women is Deborah. She wasn't just a judge but also a prophet who led Israel during a tough time. She confidently trusted God's plan, saying, *"The Lord, the God of Israel, commands you: 'Go... I will lead Sisera, the commander of Jabin's army, with his chariots and his troops to the Kishon River and give him into your hands'"* (Judges 4:6-7). Deborah teaches us how to be brave leaders, trust in God, and stand up for what's right—even when it's hard. Think about your life—are there times when you need to lean on your faith and courage to make tough decisions or help others? You've got what it takes!

Reflective Exercise: Personal Role Model Reflection

Think about a woman from the Bible whose story inspires you. What qualities did she demonstrate? How did her faith influence her actions? Write down how you can embody some of these qualities in your life. This exercise can help you identify role models to guide your spiritual and personal growth.

Example:

1. Consider **Mary, the mother of Jesus,** who showed incredible courage and faith when she accepted God's plan for her life.

2. How can you demonstrate courage in your own life, whether standing up for your beliefs or supporting a friend in need?

3. Reflect on how Mary's story inspires you to trust God's plan, even when challenging.

7.5 BUILDING YOUR CHRISTIAN LEGACY

Understanding Your Unique Influence

Your legacy isn't just about what you accomplish; it's about how you make others feel and how you bring Christ's love into every interaction. Think about the impact you want to have on those around you. What values do you want to be known for? How can you show God's love in your daily actions? Your legacy is built one choice at a time, so start making intentional decisions that reflect your faith and values.

Modern Example: Consider Sarah, a 15-year-old who started a "Kindness Club" at her school. The club focuses on performing random acts of kindness, from writing encouraging notes to teachers to organizing community clean-up days. Sarah's initiative has created a ripple effect, inspiring others to act with kindness and compassion, reflecting her desire to leave a legacy of love and service.

Creating a Legacy Journal

Have you ever thought about how your everyday choices shape who you are and the legacy you'll leave behind? A great way to reflect on this is by starting a "Legacy Journal." Use it to document the choices you make each day that reflect your values and faith. Maybe you showed kindness to someone who needed it, stood up for what was right, or supported a friend through a tough time. These small but powerful moments all contribute to the legacy you're building.

Your Legacy Journal can be a personal space to track your growth—physically, emotionally, and spiritually. Write down what you did, how it made you feel, and what you learned. For instance, if you helped a friend in need, you could write about the situation, your feelings at the time, and how it made you feel afterwards. Did stepping out of your comfort zone to help someone make you feel more confident? Did standing up for someone remind you of how strong you are?

As you journal, look back at your entries and reflect on how much you've grown. You'll see kindness, courage, and faith patterns shaping your life. The more you reflect, the more you can continue to build a legacy of love, service, and faith—qualities that will inspire others and strengthen your sense of who you are.

As we conclude this chapter, remember, leadership isn't about having a title or position. As you continue to grow and learn, authentic leadership is about living out your faith with love, courage, and integrity and inspiring others to do the same. You don't have to wait to be an adult to be a leader. You're already leading through your everyday choices, acts of kindness, and moments of bravery. Your Legacy Journal will be a powerful reminder that leadership starts now in the daily small but meaningful decisions you make. So, what kind of legacy will you begin today? Start one entry at a time, and watch how you grow!

ACTIVITY - CHAPTER 7

Scan the QR code

Bonus Chapter: Embracing Diversity: Living Out Faith in a Global Community

STEP INTO A WORLD OF FAITH AND DIVERSITY

I magine stepping into a world filled with vibrant colors, sounds, and expressions—each one unique, beautiful, and important. Just like this fantastic world, Christianity isn't one single, uniform experience. It's more like a rich tapestry woven from countless traditions, cultures, and expressions of faith. This diversity makes Christianity beautiful and allows you to see how God works through different people and places.

As you grow spiritually, learning to understand and embrace this diversity can deepen your relationship with God. You don't have to fit into one specific mold or follow just one way of expressing your faith—there's a path that's uniquely yours in His grand story. Whether through the way you worship, your prayers, or how you show love to others, your relationship with God is personal and unique.

In this chapter, we will explore how you can celebrate the diversity of faith, build empathy for others, and make a meaningful impact in the world, all while staying true to your beliefs. Think about the friends you have or the people you meet who might practice their faith differently from you—there's so much you can learn from them! By opening your heart and mind to how people experience God, you can grow spiritually and build stronger, more meaningful relationships.

Celebrating diversity is about seeing the value in everyone's story, not just your own. It's about understanding that we all have different journeys, making the body of Christ unique. Empathy helps you put yourself in someone else's shoes, listen to their experiences, and learn from them. As you do this, you'll be making a real difference—not only in your life but in the lives of others, too.

Your Unique Path

Remember: Your faith journey is personal. You don't have to follow the same path as everyone else. Just as each color adds something special to a painting, your unique experiences and expressions of faith add something beautiful to the bigger picture. So, embrace the diversity around you, learn from others, and allow your heart to be open to all the incredible ways God works in your life and those around you.

What steps can you take to celebrate this diversity? How can you build empathy and understanding in your relationships with others? As we dive into this chapter, let's explore how you can walk your unique path rooted in faith while making a meaningful impact. The journey is yours—how will you make it extraordinary?

8.1 Celebrating Diversity in Faith: Discovering the Beauty of Global Christianity

When you think of Christianity, you might picture your church's services, how your family prays, or the traditions you know. But did you know Christians worldwide worship God in many different, beautiful ways? Imagine stepping into a world where worship might mean quietly gathering in homes for prayer or joyfully dancing and singing during a service. Each style of worship is a unique expression of God's love and grace, and exploring these differences can help you see how vast and vibrant His family is. This diversity in worship is not just a reflection of culture, but a celebration of the many ways we can connect with God.

For example, the Ethiopian Orthodox Church celebrates ancient rituals passed down for centuries, while in Brazil, Pentecostal churches come alive with dance and music that express the joy of knowing Jesus. In South Korea, many Christians rise early for morning prayers, starting their day with quiet reflection and focus on God. These traditions aren't just different—they reflect the richness of Christianity across cultures, each one showing us a new aspect of God's character.

Personal Story: Emily's Discovery

A 15-year-old from Texas, Emily joined a two-week youth exchange program with a Christian family in Kenya. She was amazed by the joyful worship she experienced there. "Their church services were so energetic, with singing and dancing. It showed me that there are so many ways to connect with God. I realized I could bring more joy into my worship," she shared.

Interactive Challenge: Cultural Exploration

Are you ready to explore the world of Christianity beyond your own experience? Try this Cultural Exploration Challenge! Each month, pick a new Christian tradition from a different part of the world to learn about. You can dive into its history, listen to its music, try cooking a traditional dish, or even watch videos of its worship online. Keep a journal to reflect on what you learn and how these new insights impact your faith. It isn't just about learning new things—it's about seeing the beauty of how Christians connect with God.

8.2 BUILDING EMPATHY AND UNDERSTANDING: THE HEART OF FAITH

Faith is not just about what we believe; it's about how we live it out by showing kindness, understanding, and empathy to others. Jesus teaches us to love our neighbors, which means *everyone*—not just people who look, think, or worship like us.

Building empathy starts with listening and engaging with people from different backgrounds at school or in your community. Ask them about their experiences, listen to their stories, and try to see the world from their perspective. You don't have to agree with everything, but showing respect and kindness builds bridges. When you understand someone else's challenges and joys, you start to reflect the love of Jesus more fully. This journey of understanding and empathy is not just about others, but about your own personal growth and the deepening of your faith.

Personal Testimonial: Isabella's Journey

Isabella, a 17-year-old from New York, worked on a class project with students from different religious backgrounds. "At first, I was unsure about how to connect with them," she said. "but when I listened to their stories and shared mine, I realized our differences were beautiful. We had so much to learn from each other. It made me want to be more understanding and kind as Jesus taught us." **This sharing of experiences and learning from each other is what builds a strong, empathetic community.**

Take a moment to think about a time when you felt different or misunderstood. How did that make you feel? Now, imagine someone else feeling the same way. Write your thoughts in your journal, and ask yourself: How can you use your experiences to make others feel more welcome and understood? What can you do this week to reach out to someone who might feel left out? Consider talking to someone new, listening to their story, and showing the same love and kindness that Jesus showed to everyone He met.

8.3 PRAYING FOR THE WORLD: CONNECTING THROUGH PRAYER

Prayer is one of the most powerful ways we can connect with God and people worldwide. When you pray for others—especially those facing tough challenges like poverty, persecution, or natural disasters—you show God in action. Your prayers can bring hope, comfort, and strength to people you may never meet.

To get started, **create a global prayer calendar!** Choose a different country or issue to focus on each day of the week. For example, on Monday, pray for peace in conflict zones, and on Tuesday, lift people who lack clean water. You could also join global prayer events, like the World Day of Prayer, where people from over 170 countries gather to pray for critical international issues. Imagine being part of something so big and impactful, even from your room.

Personal Story: Aiden's Prayer Journey

Aiden, a 16-year-old, felt called to start a global prayer initiative with his youth group after learning about Christians struggling in other parts of the world. "I made a prayer calendar and prayed for a different country each day," "Aiden said. "It opened our eyes to the needs of others, and it brought us closer as a group. It felt like we were part of something much bigger than ourselves."

Sample Prayer for Your Journal

You can use a prayer like this to start your global prayer journey:

"Dear Heavenly Father, I lift my brothers and sisters worldwide who face hardship and persecution. Please give them strength, comfort, and hope. Help me remember them in my prayers, and show me how to support them. In Jesus name, Amen."

8.4 SERVICE: MAKING A DIFFERENCE CLOSE TO HOME AND FAR AWAY

Service isn't just about big, dramatic projects—it's about the small, everyday acts of kindness that can have a considerable impact. Whether helping a new student feel welcome or organizing a small fundraiser for a cause you care about, every act of service reflects God.

Get Started with a Service Project:

1. **Identify a Need:** Look around your community or school for an area where you can help.

2. **Gather a Team:** Invite friends to join you—working together is more fun and effective!

3. **Plan and Act:** Whether it's a clean-up project, a bake sale for charity, or volunteering at a local shelter, take small steps toward making a difference.

Personal Story: Naomi's Initiative

Naomi, a high school junior, saw a need in her community and took action. "Here was a local shelter that needed supplies, so I organized a drive at my school," she said. "I collected clothes, toiletries, and food. It was amazing to see everyone come together to help. It reminded me of how powerful small acts of kindness can be."

8.5 SHARING YOUR FAITH WITH RESPECT AND SENSITIVITY

Sharing your faith is one of the most powerful ways to show God's love, but it's important to do so with kindness and respect. Everyone's journey is different, and everyone's story matters. When you share, remember to listen, too. Share your own experiences, but also be open to hearing about others'. Ask questions, not to argue, but to learn and understand. True conversations about faith are rooted in **love, not debate.**

Role-Playing Exercise: Practice Sharing Faith

With a friend, practice sharing your faith respectfully and sensitively. Take turns playing different roles and giving each other feedback. This exercise helps build confidence and teaches you to share your beliefs with grace, understanding, and love.

8.6 UNITY IN DIVERSITY: FINDING STRENGTH IN DIFFERENCES

Christianity is like a beautifully woven tapestry, where every thread represents a different culture, tradition, and expression of faith. When we celebrate these differences, we find strength in unity. By focusing on what unites us—our shared love for Christ—we build a stronger, more welcoming community that reflects the kingdom.

How Can You Promote Unity?

You can join or start a multicultural club or event at your school, celebrate different traditions, and find ways to serve together. When we appreciate the diversity in the body of Christ, we create a place where everyone feels valued.

Conclusion: Embrace Your Role in God's Global Family

As you finish this chapter, remember you are part of something bigger than yourself. You belong to a global family of believers who express their faith in countless ways. Embrace this diversity, learn from it, and let it deepen your love for God and others. Every step you take toward understanding and respecting different cultures brings you closer to heart, which cherishes diversity and unity.

Call to Action: Make a Difference Today!

How will you embrace diversity and make a difference this week? Whether it's learning about a new culture, starting a prayer calendar, or planning a service project, take action! Your faith journey uniquely connects you to God's vibrant, global family. Let's celebrate this beautiful diversity together!

FINAL ACTIVITY

Scan the QR code

Conclusion

As we come to the end of our shared adventure in *Sparkle & Shine: Teen Devotional for Girls,* let's take a moment to reflect on the transformative journey we've traveled together. Each page of this book was thoughtfully crafted to empower incredible teen girls like you, equipping you to face life's challenges with unwavering faith and growing confidence. We've explored how to rise above peer pressure, manage anxiety, and embrace God's boundless love for you every day.

Our mission has been to provide you with a trusted guide—a companion on your journey through the complexities of adolescence—reminding you of your invaluable worth in Christ. We've discussed building healthy relationships, managing life's pressures with peace, and seeing your unique beauty and purpose through God's eyes.

Remember, each of you is deeply loved and valued by God. His presence is with you always, empowering you to face each day with love, strength, and confidence. The journey is just beginning, and **with God by your side, there is nothing you cannot overcome.**

GO OUT INTO THE WORLD, SPARKLE WITH HIS LOVE, AND SHINE WITH HIS GRACE!

A Prayer for Guidance and Strength

"Dear Lord, I pray for every girl reading this devotional and all teens worldwide. Thank You for their unique journeys. Guide, protect, and fill them with Your wisdom as they navigate their teenage years. Help them remember they are never alone and deeply loved by You.

Give them strength in their faith and joy in their daily lives. Let them shine with Your love, becoming lights in their communities. Equip them to face each day with confidence, knowing they are cherished by You.

In Jesus' name, Amen."

We'd Love Your
Feedback!

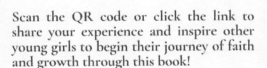

Scan the QR code or click the link to share your experience and inspire other young girls to begin their journey of faith and growth through this book!

THANK YOU!

References

20 Encouraging Bible Verses about Our Identity in Christ
https://www.biblestudytools.com/topical-verses/bible-verses-about-our-identity-in-christ/

How Using Social Media Affects Teenagers
https://childmind.org/article/how-using-social-media-affects-teenagers/

5 Women of the Bible Who Make Good Role Models
https://aop.com/blogs/lesson-plans/5-women-of-the-bible-who-make-good-role-models

9 ways to help teens with body image issues
https://www.counselling-directory.org.uk/blog/2019/05/15/9-ways-to-help-teens-with-body-image-issues

3 Friendships in the Bible and What They Teach Us
https://www.jesusfilm.org/blog/friendships-in-bible/

Seven Biblical Steps to Resolving Conflict | Pastors.com
https://blog.pastors.com/articles/seven-biblical-steps-to-resolving-conflict/

How to Set Biblical Boundaries as a Christian
https://equippinggodlywomen.com/community/christian-boundaries/

The Benefits of Mentorship in the Christian Faith - Dominion TV
https://dominiontv.net/the-benefits-of-mentorship-in-the-christian-faith-growing-together/

21 Bible Verses to Calm Anxiety
https://www.ramseysolutions.com/personal-growth/bible-verses-for-anxiety

13 Practical Time Management Skills To Teach Teens
https://lifeskillsadvocate.com/blog/13-practical-time-management-skills-to-teach-teens/

How Doubt Can Deepen Your Faith
https://www.cru.org/storylines/2020/september/how-doubt-can-deepen-your-faith

16 Bible Stories About Fear
https://coffeewithstarla.com/ways-to-deal-with-fear-in-your-life/

Devotions for Teenagers and Youth - Daily devotions for youth ...
https://studentdevos.com/

What does the Bible say about the power of words?
https://www.gotquestions.org/power-of-words.html

How To Use Social Media As A Christian Teen - Axis.org
https://axis.org/blog/how-to-use-social-media-as-a-christian-teen/#:~:text=Using%20Social%20Media%20as%20a,kindness%2C%20love%2C%20and%20understanding.

50 Community Service Ideas for Teen Volunteers
https://www.teenlife.com/blog/50-community-service-ideas-teen-volunteers/

Can Religion Help the Teen Mental Health Crisis? | Essay
https://www.zocalopublicsquare.org/2022/11/14/religion-teen-mental-health/ideas/essay/

10 Powerful Bible Verses for Depression and Anxiety
https://www.cassidysheart.com/10-powerful-bible-verses-for-depression-and-anxiety/

What Does the Bible Say About Self-Care? (A Christian ...
https://equippinggodlywomen.com/faith/christian-self-care/

What does the Bible say about overcoming grief?
https://www.gotquestions.org/overcoming-grief.html

What is biblical womanhood?
https://www.gotquestions.org/biblical-womanhood.html

Do You Have to 'Love' Your Body? A Christian Perspective ...
https://comparedtowho.me/christian-perspective-on-body-positivity/

The 10 Virtues of a Proverbs 31 Woman
https://avirtuouswoman.org/10-virtues-of-the-proverbs-31-woman/

Ten Women Leaders in the Bible
https://influencemagazine.com/Practice/Ten-Women-Leaders-in-the-Bible

How to Study the Bible: 8 Key Tips Teens Need to Know
https://churchleaders.com/youth/youth-leaders-articles/320350-teaching-teens-read-bible-actually-understand.html

Benefits of Keeping a Prayer Journal
https://rachelwojo.com/benefits-of-keeping-a-prayer-journals/

Teens and Spiritual Gifts: How to Help Discover Them
https://churchleaders.com/youth/youth-leaders-articles/345842-teens-and-spiritual-gifts-how-to-help-discover-them.html

5 Reasons Every Teenager Should Go On a Mission Trip
https://youthworks.com/blog/5-reasons-every-teenager-should-go-on-a-mission-trip/#:~:text=Mission%20Trips%20Broaden%20Perspectives%20for%20Teenagers.
Pulling%20teenagers%20from%20their%20typical,context%20comes%20into%20truer%20focus.

Setting Goals to Fulfill Your God-Given Purpose
https://www.focusonthefamily.com/faith/setting-goals-to-fulfill-your-god-given-purpose/

How to Choose a College ... and Keep Your Faith
https://intervarsity.org/news/how-to-choose-a-college-and-keep-your-faith

Eight Practical Ways You Can Integrate Your Faith into ...
https://ronkelleher.com/547-eight-practical-ways-you-can-integrate-your-faith-into-your-workplace/

10 Financial Principles That Are Biblical
https://www.backtothebible.org/post/10-financial-principles-that-are-biblical

Made in the USA
Monee, IL
12 December 2024

73631454R00066